BEFORE THE IVY

BEFORE THE IVY

THE CUBS' GOLDEN AGE IN PRE-WRIGLEY CHICAGO

LAURENT PERNOT

University of Illinois Press

URBANA, CHICAGO, AND SPRINGFIELD

Frontispiece: The White Stockings' championship
squad of the mid-1880s. (Author's collection)

Library of Congress Cataloging-in-Publication Data
Pernot, Laurent.
Before the ivy : the Cubs' golden age in
pre-Wrigley Chicago / Laurent Pernot.
pages cm
Includes bibliographical references and index.
ISBN 978-0-252-08028-9 (pbk. : alk. paper) —
ISBN 978-0-252-09665-5 (e-book)
1. Chicago Cubs (Baseball team)—History.
2. Wrigley Field (Chicago, Ill.)—History.
I. Title.
GV875.C6P47   2015
796.357'640977311—dc23   2014011264

To my grandfather Marcel Thiebaud,
who gave me my love of history,
and to Al Broten, who taught me about baseball
and whose only flaw was to be a Sox fan.

To my sons, may they stay true to their passions.

CONTENTS

INTRODUCTION

MORE THAN A CENTURY AFTER their last victory in the World Series, the Chicago Cubs' best chance at renewed glory may be a Field of Dreams–like lesson with their predecessors on the West Side of Chicago at Polk and Wood, where one can still stand over part of the old outfield.

Before the ballpark that would become Wrigley Field and be symbolized by its ivy,[1] Chicago was home to a combination of league builders, sports entrepreneurs, and Hall of Famers with no equals before and few since.

Prior to its move to the North Side in 1916, the team appeared in four of the first seven World Series, winning two. The Cubs have appeared in just six of the more than one hundred World Series played since, and won just one postseason series, in 2003.

Until the Seattle Mariners tied the record in 2001, the 1906 West Side Cubs were sole owners of the all-time mark for most wins in one season, with 116 in 1906. They still boast the best winning percentage ever, as they reached the mark in just 152 games, compared to Seattle's 162. The skippers with the three highest winning percentages in team history are Albert Spalding, Adrian "Cap" Anson, and Frank Chance, none of whom ever managed at Wrigley Field. The legendary Tinker-to-Evers-to-Chance triple-play combination never plied its trade on the North Side.

No Cub has recorded more hits, singles, doubles, or RBIs over a Cubs career than Anson. Mordecai "Three Finger" Brown still holds the single-season team records in earned run average (1.04) and all-time record for shutouts (48). Frank Chance remains the only Cubs player to steal four hundred bases. Al Spalding still reigns as the pitcher with the best win-loss record in the history of baseball (.795). Other pre–Wrigley Field Cubs still own single-season team records for wins and strikeouts by a pitcher, on-base percentage, batting average, triples, walks, and stolen bases.

Most team histories begin in 1876 with the newly created National League—and the team's victory of the first-ever NL pennant—but the team's roots go all the way back to the late 1860s. The early 1870s—when the then–White Stockings played downtown and then on the South Side—brought many successes, though the "Chicago nine" was denied two championship titles early in that decade, one owing to league infighting and the other to the Great Chicago Fire.

The dozen years beginning in 1880 was the greatest period in team history, with eleven top-three finishes and five pennants won in ballparks located on the site of today's Andrew Jackson Language Academy, at Congress and Loomis, and where Millennium Park presently sits. The team then spent most of the 1890s and early 1900s way out of contention, under such names as Colts, Orphans, and Remnants.

The lowest point in team history up to that point came in 1901, when the Remnants limped to a .381 winning percentage. That record low would hold for more than fifty years and remains the fifth-worst on the club's all-time list, with the most recent lower point being the .377 outcome in 2012.

As the team rebuilt with young players, the name Cubs began to take hold, although the *Chicago Tribune* tried unsuccessfully to popularize the moniker Spuds in reference to the team's Irish owner. Fans should take heart: Within two years of their disastrous 1901 campaign, the team had a winning record and by 1906 went to the World Series on the heels of a .763 season. Though they lost that duel to the White Sox, the Cubs would win the next two against the Tigers. After a few more years of close contention, and an unsuccessful World Series run in 1910, the team ran into athletic and financial trouble and moved north after the 1915 season. (A decade-by-decade overview of team results appears in the appendix.)

Beyond titles and feats on the field, nineteenth-century Chicago played a key role in the professionalization of baseball, modern sports journalism, and the ascendancy of management over players, as orchestrated by Chicagoan William Hulbert, father of the National League and owner of its Chicago franchise, and Rockford-area native Al Spalding, of pitching, managing, and sports-empire fame. The race and class issues the broader country was facing found their way onto the field as well, the sport reflecting society's broader struggles.

It turns out that history does repeat itself in some regards, as for a brief spell in the early 1870s, a *Chicago Tribune* official presided over the Chicago Base Ball Association, and controversies between team owners and rooftop owners beyond the outfield walls surfaced in the early 1900s. We may even owe the idiom "out in left field" to the team's West Side Grounds. And, though the White Sox enjoy bragging rights for winning the only Chicago vs. Chicago World Series, they inherited the Cubs' old name and were even preceded by the National League franchise at 35th and Wentworth.

Sadly, beyond shaping so much of the Sox's identity, the enduring legacy of the early Cubs was not winning, but being lovable and profitable losers. More than the famous goat, that may be the franchise's true curse, a theory that's not altogether out in left field.

FROM LITTLE ENGLISH ACORN
TO GIANT AMERICAN OAK

ON A COLD AND FOGGY LONDON DAY in March 1889, a group of American baseball stars played an exhibition game before Edward, Prince of Wales and future King of England, and hundreds of curious nobles and onlookers. The affair had been arranged by A. G. Spalding, perhaps the game's greatest early promoter, who painstakingly explained the game's subtleties to the prince. Though excited by the action on the field, the monarch concluded, "I consider Base Ball an excellent game, but Cricket a better one."[1]

The goal of the exhibition, which marked the end of a world tour by Spalding and assorted stars, had been to give "the masses everywhere an opportunity to witness a pastime peculiarly American." The prince's statement, reported by several newspapers, was an affront made all the more stinging to Spalding in that he had dedicated himself to erasing baseball's British roots.

In his 1911 autobiography, Spalding would proclaim baseball to be "the exponent of American Courage, Confidence, Combativeness; American Dash, Discipline, Determination; American Energy, Eagerness, Enthusiasm; American Pluck, Persistency, Performance; American Spirit, Sagacity, Success; American Vim, Vigor, Virility."[2]

To be sure, teams in the 1850s and '60s had stressed values like practice and teamwork over natural ability.[3] But the above virtues were carefully chosen by Spalding as part of a well-orchestrated propaganda effort to rewrite the history of the sport as "of modern and purely American origin."[4]

The Chicagos and the All-Americas teams surround Al Spalding, top hat in hand, in Leighton, England, during their great world tour of 1888–1889. Spalding's plan to export baseball fell short, but it generated much publicity back home for the young sport. (Author's collection)

In 1907, Spalding and a group of baseball magnates had anointed themselves as a baseball historical commission and unanimously adopted the following:

First—That Base Ball had its origins in the United States;
Second—That the first scheme for playing it, according to the best evidence obtainable to date, was devised by Abner Doubleday, at Cooperstown, New York, in 1839.[5]

The evidence that was to be studied by the commission during its historical research burned, and the above conclusion was attained on the sole basis of recollections by an aging mining engineer, Abner Graves, who had been the schoolmate of Abner Doubleday. Thus Doubleday, who would go on to fire the first Union gun at Fort Sumter, was credited with the invention of baseball in a story of biblical proportions. According to Graves, schoolboy Doubleday broke up a game of marbles to lay down the rules of the game, draw the diamond, and christen it "baseball."[6] Contradicting his own statement that a crude form of the game had been played for many years prior to 1839, Spalding capitalized on the dramatic ramifications of the Doubleday story:

> Cricket is an Athletic Sociable, played in a conventional, decorous and English manner. Base Ball is an Athletic turmoil, played and applauded in an unconventional, enthusiastic and American manner. The founder of our National Game became a Major General in the United States Army! The sport had its baptism when our country was in the preliminary agonies of a fratricidal conflict. . . . It was the medium by which, in the days following the 'late unpleasantness,' a million warriors and their sons, from both belligerent sections, passed naturally, easily, gracefully, from a state of bitter battling to one of perfect peace.[7]

Though the Doubleday story gained ground among the public—in major part because of the creationism advanced in Spalding's book—several of the game's early giants refused to go along with this myth-making, taking instead an evolutionist approach that led to England. Famed manager Branch Rickey pronounced that "the only thing Doubleday ever started was the Civil War."[8]

Henry Chadwick, whom Spalding called the "Father of the Game" and who edited A. G.'s annual baseball guide, wrote several histories of the game more rooted in fact. While he also got caught up in descriptions of baseball as the great American sport, he did trace its birth to the British Isles. As early as 1868, Chadwick published *The Game of Base Ball: How to Learn It, How to Play It, and How to Teach It*. In it, the British-born Brooklynite recalled that in the 1830s, "my favorite field game was the old school-boy sport of Rounders. We used to dig a hole in the ground for the home position and place four stones in a circle, or nearly so, for the bases, and, choosing up sides, we went in for a lively time at what was the parent game of base ball." The game was played much like modern baseball, except that fielders had to hit the runner with the ball to record an out. A successful throw of the batted ball into the hole at home would retire the side. "Of course the game was merely a source of fun and exercise, but little skill being required to play it, any school boy being able to learn it in ten minutes. But from this little English acorn of Rounders has the giant American oak of base ball grown, and as much difference exists between the British school-boy sport and our American National game, as between the seedling and the full grown king of the forest."[9]

Just like the Doubleday Genesis story, Chadwick's theory was short on real evidence. Though it did have the merit of keeping the Doubleday myth from taking too great a hold, it too has fallen by the wayside as evidence has grown of a more diffuse ancestry to the game. An 1823 letter in the *New York Advocate* referred to "base ball" being played in the city.[10] A Hall of Fame historian documented the existence of a baseball team that challenged all comers in 1825.[11] In 1833, six years before the date on which Spalding had Doubleday invent baseball, Town Ball, which Chadwick called the American equivalent of Rounders, was played in organized fashion in Philadelphia. Posts had replaced the rocks, and each player was assigned a specific position on the field. In New England, a similar game was referred to as the "Massachusetts game."[12]

In later years, historian Robert Henderson confirmed the sport's evolutionary nature when he found images of ball-and-bat games in British and American children's books from the eighteenth century.[13] As for the name of the game itself, it appears as "base-ball" in 1744's *A Pretty Little Pocket Book,* published in London. Jane Austen's 1817 *Northanger Abbey* also refers to the game.[14] Not that England had a monopoly on bat-and-ball games, which have been recorded for hundreds of years in places as far-flung as Austria, Germany, and Libya. As William Ryczek has written, had Chadwick hailed from the other side of the English Channel, he might have insisted baseball was the direct descendant of the French game tecque.[15] Cherokee Indians in the 1700s are even thought to have played a game called stickball.[16]

Like baseball itself, the obsession with the sport's origins is typically American. The Founding Fathers are so ingrained in the national psyche, and this nation of immigrants is so obsessed with roots and geneses, that Americans have written countless volumes on the subject.

Historic uncertainties aside, two things are for sure: it is in America that baseball got formalized and flourished, and it is in New York, where young men played together as the Knickerbockers, that much of the game was formalized. Though there are records of earlier games by earlier teams in that same city, the Knickerbockers alone have an uninterrupted lineage to the game as we know it today. Although the game's "modern" form would not be fully in place until the turn of the twentieth century, it was this group of self-described gentlemen—merchants and dealers for the most part—who in 1845 wrote down the rules that would form the basis for the organized play of the sport as it spread across the nation. Though Alexander Cartwright would, like Doubleday before him, get elevated to the status of Father of the Game by many, research has established that the codification of the game was a group effort and that several of his teammates played an equal if not greater role. The men eliminated the requirement that fielders hit runners with the ball (allowing for harder balls to be used for batting) and adopted the diamond, setting the diagonal distance between the bases at forty-two paces. Rule changes would continue for some time. In 1845, the Knickerbockers challenged other athletes to play a game at the Elysian Fields in Hoboken, New Jersey—and lost 23 to 1. Three-out innings and foul lines were instituted, and the game was set at nine innings, in contrast to the "Massachusetts game," which required one hundred runs to win. The new rules came to be known as the "New York game," and that version of baseball eclipsed the others.

Better defined and easier to play and follow, the game grew in popularity, and within ten years more than twenty organized teams had been assembled in New York and New England. The Knickerbockers attempted to rule the sport and resisted the spread of the game to quarters they did not deem gentlemanly enough. In 1859, the stuffy New York group was the victim of a coup when the rest of the teams created the National Association of Base Ball Players, paving the way to more open governance. By 1860, the more progressive association had swelled to sixty teams, including clubs in St. Louis and Chicago.[17]

THE BASEBALL FRONTIER

IT IS UNCLEAR WHEN ORGANIZED BASEBALL was first played in Chicago, but there is evidence of games taking place by the mid-1850s. As early as 1851, the *Lockport Telegraph* reported on a contest between the Joliet Hunkidoris and the hometown Sleepers. A Niagara Base Ball Club was reported founded in July 1818 in Chicago. The earliest remaining mention of a baseball game in the city proper appears in the August 17, 1858 edition of the *Daily Journal*. The game between the Unions and the Excelsiors was played with the same rules in place in New York; the Chicago Baseball Club—made up of a handful of local teams—held a convention on July 21 of that year to adopt that set of rules.[1] That same year, the *Chicago Tribune* reported the Unions lost to "Downer's Grove" [*sic*] at the Unions' own grounds at Harrison and Halsted. After the game, the players went to dinner and the theater in uniform.[2]

Henry Chadwick's old baseball clippings contain an intriguing undated item that some have interpreted as the account of a game between staffers for Abraham Lincoln and Stephen Douglas. Clearly from Chicago, the item is headlined "The Political Base Ball Match" and refers to a game played in front of 1,200 spectators on the grounds of the Excelsior Base Ball Club at the corner of West lake and Ann streets. The teams in the box score are listed as "Douglas" and "Lincoln." At the bottom is the following text: "There's a victory in store where Douglas will make no 'runs.' He is a lame 'short stop' and has been 'caught out.'" The bottom of the article is damaged, but these words are preceded by "Never Mind, Lincoln"; but before the text resumes there is a gap seemingly stemming from sloppy cutting with scissors, and then what looks to be the word "says." It appears the words "Lincoln" and "says" were clipped diagonally, but one cannot be sure there were no other words in between them. This could be a Lincoln quote or, more likely, just newspaper humor or an all-out parody. The "Douglas" and 'Lincoln" could simply refer to supporters of the candidates. Either way, baseball fever and political passion seem to have come together in what could have been either the 1858 race for the Illinois U.S. Senate seat or the 1860 presidential campaign.[3]

Beyond the written instructions on how to play the game, teams abided by a code of conduct that espoused middle-class and "respectable" working-class values. The Victorian concern for self-control and order would be reflected in the adoption of strict codes of conduct, punishing tardiness and profane language, and the appointment of umpires to make sure discipline prevailed on the diamond. Though they surely did not apply to all players, descriptions of baseball players as "gentlemen" who engaged in "fair play" and "genteel sportsmanship" became commonplace.[4]

The advent of the Civil War put many clubs in dormancy, including Chicago's Excelsiors.[5] Yet the war likely had a beneficial impact on the game. The U.S. Sanitary Commission listed baseball among the approved pastimes for Union troops, and a Confederate manual encouraged "manly play of ball" as part of soldiers' daily exercise routines.[6] The many Union soldiers who took to the game, be it in Confederate prison camps or during breaks in the fighting—forty thousand Northern combatants attended a game on Christmas Day 1862—came home eager to spread the new baseball "mania."[7] Guards and prisoners played or took in games together, and historian George Kirsch has argued the war's true baseball legacy was not to be found in the North but in the game's growth in the South, where it had been rare antebellum.[8]

The game grew rapidly after the conflict: from sixty teams in five states in 1860, the National Association of Base Ball Players had grown to 202 clubs in seventeen states by 1866.[9]

On August 17, 1865, the *Chicago Daily Republican* proclaimed:

The old Excelsior ball Club, which a few years was one of the institutions of our city, has been reorganized and hereafter will be willing to meet all comers. The club was organized in 1857 and for three years played regularly and became known as one of the best clubs in the west. After the breaking out of the War many of its members enlisted, and the club was thus broken up. With the return of peace the members have once more organized the old club, and now they practice regularly, twice a week on their new grounds on the corner of May and West Lake streets.... A game between two nines of the club was played yesterday afternoon, in which they showed that they have not forgotten the exercise of the club, while engaged in the use of the rifle.[10]

In 1866, thirty-two clubs were competing in the area—where play included teams like the Chicago Actives and the Evanston Gazelles and, still, was dominated by the Excelsiors[11]—enough for the *Chicago Tribune* to announce the arrival of the "Age of Baseball."[12] Increasingly, teams of gentlemen who had only scheduled games against social equals began to incorporate into the lineup any player who could boost their chances of prevailing.[13] Still, baseball in Chicago was played and hailed by businessmen, educators, journalists, and social reformers who sought good character and physical health, which was increasingly exhorted in the media. The body, when left to its own devices, became the "the casket of the mind," a preacher claimed.[14]

Beginning in the late 1860s, magnates like Marshall Field and George Pullman began to sponsor internal leagues and company teams—made up of upper-level employees rather than unskilled laborers to promote exercise and morals among their staff and, in the process, get free advertising in the newspapers.[15]

Several amateur teams evolved on the city's western edge. The Actives used a diamond at Lake and Ada and the Mutuals showcased their talents at Leavitt and Van Buren. The Libertys made their home at Madison and Western. The Excelsiors played downtown, while the Atlantics were the squad of the North Side (which ended at Division Street) and the Pastimes represented the South Side (the city ended at 12th Street). Other local entries included the Never-sweats and the Dreadnaughts. Only the Atlantics could boast of enclosed grounds in the city.[16]

By the end of the decade, there were teams throughout the state. On July 2, 1870, the *Chicago Tribune* reported on a road trip by the Garden City Baseball Club to Ottawa, Illinois, where they were to play the home team, the Shabbonas. The affair was very genteel only until the game started, but the game was a crowd-pleaser in spite, or because of it:

> They were escorted to the Clifton House, where an elegant suite of rooms was assigned them. After a substantial dinner, they proceeded to the fair grounds where a large concourse of people was assembled to witness the players.... The people seemed determined to rush up and cross the limits.... No amount of persuasion could move them. Finally four or five swift foul balls were sent with great rapidity into the mass, and the crowd quickly fell back and did not venture up. Several were injured severely.... The playing throughout was very fine, some magnificent fly catches being made on both sides.... When the result was known [31–17 for Chicago], it brought forth tremendous cheers.

The previous Wednesday, the host Empire Base Ball Club of Champaign and the Libertys of Springfield had played a game "long-talked-of" in the central part of the state, won by Springfield 73–35.[17]

Henry Chadwick attributed America's rising interest in sport in part to baseball. The great game would also boost national pride by helping Americans to step out of England's shadow once and for all.

> At that period—and it is but eleven years ago [1857]—I need not state that out-door recreation was comparatively unknown to the large mass of the American people. In fact, as is well known, we were the regular target for the shafts of raillery and even abuse from our out-door sport-loving cousins of England, in consequence of our national neglect of sports and pastimes, and our too great devotion to business and the "Almighty Dollar." But thanks to Base Ball—the entering wedge of the great reformation which has since taken place—we have been transformed into quite another people, and as we never do things by halves, but generally rush into *furores* and extremes, the chances are that from being too neglectful of out-door sports we shall become too fond of them, and, from being content to playing second fiddle to the sportsmen and athletes of England, we shall not

rest content until we have defeated them in every specialty of games, of which they have, for so many years, been the leading exemplars.[18]

Traveling teams celebrated physical fitness and prowess in contests that were followed by cohorts of reporters, and when such an event took place in Chicago in 1867, the city took notice. But, to Chadwick's horror, discussion of the game centered on gambling and cheating rather than highbrow ideals.[19]

For all of Chadwick's vigor in defending the virtue of the sport, the players in this controversial contest were no longer pure amateurs. As clubs began to draw more spectators, even when they charged admission, many baseball men were eager to cast aside the image of the gentleman-player to make more money.[20] While the National Association of Base Ball Players forbade payment of salary to any player, there was a widespread practice of hiring talented young men with the understanding they would spend little time at work and long hours on the diamond.

That is how a teenager named Albert G. Spalding left Rockford's Forest City Club in 1867, ostensibly to become a grocery clerk but in fact to play with the Chicago Excelsiors for $40 a week. When the wholesale grocery that fielded the team failed, Spalding returned to Rockford and his old team, becoming employed in the insurance office of that club's secretary.[21]

Gambling on the game was rampant. That same year, a game between Philadelphia's Athletics and the Brooklyn Atlantics saw $10,000 change hands. Chadwick described how "men could be seen pushing along the edge of the crowd, holding hundred dollar bills, calling their bets" and concluded, sadly, that "base ball in some instances has been brought down to the level of 'Hippodrome races,' in which it is an understood thing before hand, that the horse on which the most money has been invested to win, shall be the losing horse."[22]

The *Illinois State Journal* wrote about the White Stockings of 1871:

This club has, doubtless, been re-organized on a thorough gambling basis, to be used like a race-horse or a bull terrier on the hands of experienced sportsmen, for the purpose of making money. The respectable public should give no countenance to the game of base ball when it is perverted to such bad ends. It is a rare and healthy sport when indulged in only for the pleasure and exercise which it gives to the players. But when degraded

WHEN GAMBLING CONTROLLED

Spalding used this drawing in *America's National Game* to illustrate the state of baseball before he and others cleaned up the game. (Author's collection)

to the level of the cock-pit and scrub-race course, it is no longer worthy or deserving of patronage. Let there be proper discrimination made by the public between gambling base ball and sporting base ball.[23]

This was easier said than done. The *Western Monthly* wrote about the intense involvement of the fans—both emotionally and monetarily: "Every good play on either side is hailed with huzzas, partly from amateurs who admire the feat, but chiefly from bettors who have put money on the player's side."[24]

As time went on, newspapers would treat the game, gambling, and game-fixing as parts of the same event. The *Evening Mail*'s sports reporter told how the Chicago team threw a game to prolong a series against Washington and ensure each team more gate receipts: "According to previous arrangement, the Chicago base ball club was yesterday beaten again. . . . It is astonishing, that young men will still be found so confiding as to bet on the result of a game. . . . when it is already decided by the managers."[25]

Before long, gambling accounts would dominate baseball writing, in sharp contrast with the lofty ideals and associated profits hailed by the elites who ran the sport. On July 2, 1875, Jennie Hulbert, whose husband William presided over the Chicago baseball team, wrote to a family member, "the city celebrate[s] Monday—but we as a family, tomorrow, taking a baseball game with the St. Louis, as the foundation of our *patriotism* [her underline]. I am afraid the weather will interfere with the gate receipts—if not the game."[26] On that very same day, the *Chicago Tribune*'s only report on the upcoming game consisted of telling readers that "betting here rules irregular, some betters giving odds on the Browns, while others are taking bets even. Considerable interest is manifested as to the result of the two next games."[27]

CHICAGO'S HIRED GUNS

AFTER THE CIVIL WAR, in 1866 and 1867, the reconstituted Chicago Excelsiors won tournaments against some of the best teams in the region and the Midwest, giving rise to hopes of contending at the national level. But when Washington's Nationals came to town on July 27, 1867, the locals were humiliated 49 to 4.[1] On June 21, 1868, the Cincinnati Red Stockings crushed the Excelsiors 43 to 22 and, the next day, disposed of the Atlantics 28 to 9.[2] These newly arranged Red Stockings were revolutionizing organized baseball, disorganized as it was.

In 1868, what Spalding would later call "the roundabout schemes that were being worked out in all large cities to secure good players" were cast aside by Cincinnati lawyer Aaron Champion, who turned his local club into the first professional team, the Cincinnati Red Stockings, through an $11,000 stock issue. Though not the first to be compensated to play baseball, the Cincinnati players were the first to sign contracts for the length of the season; by 1869 the total payroll approached $10,000.[3] Led by Harry Wright, the future Boston baseball magnate, the team crisscrossed the country and could not be beaten, compiling a 56-0 record, with one tie. More than two hundred thousand people saw them play.[4] The team helped spread not only the baseball gospel but professionalism, as cities throughout the country organized paid squads to face them.[5] In 1870, the Red Stockings won their first twenty-seven games before losing their first contest since 1868 to the Brooklyn Atlantics.[6] The fallen Goliath lost many of its followers after the defeat, but it was not until a late-season trip to Chicago in 1870 that the Cincinnati experiment would come crashing down.

Just a year prior, at least in the eyes of the New York press, Chicago had not been not a contender: "the Excelsiors may be doing something to bring up the club to first-class playing merit; but, if so, they are doing their work very quietly." It would take another Chicago crew to answer the call. Made up of mercenaries from across the country, the Chicago White Stockings had been organized for the express purpose of avenging the city's earlier humiliation at the hand of the Red Stockings and affirming Chicago's superiority over its midwestern neighbor. The commitment of Chicago's civic and business leaders was evident: businessman Potter Palmer was president, and former Lieutenant General Philip Sheridan and sleeping-car inventor George Pullman were vice presidents. The first meeting to organize the team was held on October 2, 1869. Soon, enough stock was sold to engage in a bidding war with existing teams and assemble the most expensive team in the country, with a payroll of $18,000, nearly double the Red Stockings' payroll. *The Cincinnati Commercial* summed it up: "It vexes the metropolitan soul of Chicago that a village like Cincinnati should bear off the palm in the baseball world."[7]

By the spring of 1870, the team some had come to call the Chicagos was one of only five teams nationwide with Cincinnati, New York, Louisville, and Baltimore to have offered their players formal contracts. But clubs in Brooklyn, Boston, and Washington also paid their players, in the form of shares of gate receipts or shadow jobs.[8] The Chicago entry soon earned the nickname of White Stockings for the white hose sported by the players to match their white flannel caps, white shirts, and blue trousers, chosen to contrast with the Red Stockings.[9]

The assemblage of former rivals from around the country on the White Stockings squad made for a lack of cohesion and some friction, which Chicago papers blasted as a poor reflection on the team and, by extension, the city. At the time, a rule allowed a sort of pinch runner who actually stood by the batter and ran in his stead at the crack of the bat. To make a point about the team's poor attitude, a Chicago newspaper mentioned that each prima donna wanted others to run for him. But it did not keep the team from trampling all in its wake on its first extended road trip, which included romps in New Orleans and Memphis. But they had yet to play the only nine that really mattered, the Red Stockings. So far, the rivalry was played out in the papers, with the *Tribune* pointing out that Chicago beat the New Orleans Atlantics 51–0 when Cincinnati had "only" beaten the Louisiana locals 36–6 a few days earlier. The Cincinnati papers countered by pointing out that the Red Stockings had at least not lowered themselves to playing on a Sunday while down South (even as the road trip proved to be a money-loser for the team), while Chicago happily obliged.[10]

Teams in Boston and in upstate New York were soon added to the list of Chicago's victims, but before they even got to the Reds, the 30-0 White Stockings got taken down by the Brooklyn Atlantics on July 4 in front of eight thousand people in New York. A New York paper concluded that "Chicago had not yet outgrown New York in any particular—save boastfulness." The team lost again to the New York Mutuals and the Philadelphia Athletics. A new streak of six victories could not erase the sting of a 9–0 loss at home to the Mutuals on July 23. Chicago fans and the media, spoiled by some early victories by a total of 150 runs, turned on the team. The *Republican* judged it "damned by four fifths of the people of Chicago."[11]

By the time the White Stockings finally took on the Reds in the fall, the anticipation still ran high. The Reds lost to the White Stockings 10–6 in Ohio in September. Some Cincinnati papers attributed the Reds' loss to a biased umpire and the absence of one of the team's stars, George Wright, and were thirsty for revenge.[12] The rematch in Chicago drew eighteen thousand—including fans who had traveled from as far as New York and Minnesota—at Dexter Park, a working racetrack located at Halsted and 42nd streets that was home to some of Chicago amateur baseball outfits in the 1860s and had been retrofitted to accommodate up to thirty thousand people on game days. In June, the team had abandoned Ogden Park, where it played previously, for the new ballpark that, while it was well beyond the city's limits, could be reached by special trains. Other fans made their way by road, creating "a continuous caravan of vehicles and dust."[13] When the ballpark was not used for games or races, Chicagoans could head to Dexter Park to partake in the popular pastime of pigeon shooting.[14]

For the two games in Chicago against the Reds—dubbed "The War of the Stockings" by the *Chicago Tribune*—the diamond was placed near the racetrack's rudimentary grandstand, and thousands of fans stood behind a rope on the edge of the infield and outfield. In Cincinnati, large crowds were

Dexter Park was the Chicago White Stockings' first home. The race-track's oval is shown on the upper left in this detail of an 1874 aerial map of the city. (Library of Congress, LC-DIG-ppmsca-08968)

gathered around the newspaper's office to catch bulletins as they came in. Now, with Wright on the field and an agreed-upon umpire to call the game, the uncontestable contest between Chicago and the "Porkopolis pets" could begin. Fifteen thousand fans were on hand, including several hundred who had come to Chicago from Cincinnati, and $20,000 in bets was said to have changed hands. In the first inning, the *Tribune* wrote, "The king of all boss-tossers, the champion batter of America, came to the plate to show Chicago that he had not been overrated. George dispatched a savage grounder to Levi Meyerle, who was on his taps for such occurrences, and Andy Leonard, who had been allowed to run the bases for Wright, was saved that trouble for the time." Then in the sixth, with the game tied at 1-1, "Harry Wright came to the bat the excitement was intense, but the crowd was as silent as a grave." Wright kicked off a four-run inning for the Reds, who were still up 5-2 at the top of eighth. As the light faded, fielding became a bit of a guessing game, and it was all tied up, 8-8, after a 6-3 inning for the White Stockings. Chicago's onslaught even forced a rare pitching change that only brought more hits and the return of the original pitcher in the ninth, only to switch again for the original replacement in the face of futility. The *Tribune* reporter, caught in the euphoria, attributed Jimmy Wood's fly-out to end the eight-run top of the ninth to Wood's desire to ensure the official win by ending the inning early. Wright, who would come to the plate in every inning, was held to two hits, and Chicago took the game 16-13. The *Tribune*'s postgame analysis the next day declared: "The friends of the Red Stockings claim that the nine is pre-eminently strong when it comes to uphill work. Here was a chance to test their climbing abilities, and if the stuff was in them, never had they better opportunity to bring it out. Alas! The demand was great but the supply poor. . . . The White Stockings. . . . constituted. . . . the strongest team in the country."[15] A day later yet, the *Tribune* again devoted nearly two full columns to the game, breathlessly declaring, "Two months ago the Reds and Whites occupied the extreme of the ladder of fame. . . . To-day, however, the Chicago nine is the first in the land. . . . She organized a nine to defeat every other in the country, more especially the Red Stockings, and she has succeeded in the undertaking."[16]

In Cincinnati, meanwhile, the *Gazette* reported, "We were beaten! We know, we feel it, how could we help it? The umpire was against us, the weather was against us, the crowd was against us, the heavens were against us, the pestilential air was against us, the Chicago nine was against us, and last, but not least, the score was against us."[17]

Given the fickle nature of Chicago's fans, the win likely had just saved professional baseball in the city. The White Stockings were again the darlings of the fair-weather fans. Chicago indeed had been dominating over the

1870 campaign: it had gone 19-7 in games against other professional teams, and 62-7 overall. The average score was 34–10, and eight players hit .350 or better, including four .400 hitters. Yet the season would end on a sour note. All year, teams played each other willy-nilly by invitation, and there was no set schedule. Rivals for the loosely defined "championship" did not even play the same number of games. The season ended in controversy after an aborted final showdown between Chicago and the New York Mutuals resulted in each team claiming the title, though others also could make a reasonable case that they also deserved it. On November 4, the two teams were scheduled to meet in Cincinnati but the game was cancelled. The *Chicago Tribune* dutifully reported the reason to its readers: "After their fearful defeat by the Reds on Wednesday, the Mutuals seem to have concluded that the West is a bad place for New York ball-tossers, and they took the first train home." A key point of contention was whether the last two completed games between Chicago and the Mutuals were "exhibition" or "regular" contests. The *New York Clipper* awarded the pennant to Chicago: "They were 'regular contests' beyond a doubt. . . . The Whites are Champion, and the fact cannot be rubbed out."[18] However, in the absence of a true league that could serve as a final authority, the matter was never settled.

While the Reds could still boast they had won sixty-eight of their seventy-five games on the year, the early glow was gone, and their own fickle fans turned on them. The *Tribune*'s special dispatch from Cincinnati on the day of the Red Stockings' loss at Chicago called the time of death: "Porkopolis disowns the Red Legs. The orphanage dates from the reception of the last inning. The yell of agonized woe . . . would not have done discredit to the lost in the infernal regions. . . . It was well for the Reds they were not here." Even Cincinnati's *Commercial* gave Chicago its due: "The White Stockings are the first club in the United States to win two games from the Reds. . . . The Chicagoans [are] the champions of the country." The Reds were disbanded at the conclusion of the season, having failed to turn a profit. In 1871, the club would return to amateurism. Wright would then take his professional endeavor to Boston, bringing with him the team's name and recruiting Spalding from Rockford in the process.[19]

In spite of these early hiccups, to baseball men like Spalding, professionalization was a welcome and irreversible process: "Genuine lovers of the sport, who admired the game for its real worth as an entertaining pastime and invigorating form of exercise, saw in the triumphs of the Reds the dawn of a new era in Base Ball; for they were forced, *nolens volens,* to recognize that professionalism had come to stay; that by it the game would be presented in its highest state of perfection; that amateurs, devoting the greater portion of their time to other pursuits, could not hope to compete with those whose business it was to play the game—and play it as a business."[20]

The White Stockings' financial results were more mixed than their play on the field. The team was popular but management could not capitalize on it. One contest against Fort Wayne in June 1870 brought $5,000 to the club.[21] Yet, there was a shake-up in leadership in July, and the shareholders meeting in early January 1871 explained why: The club was $3,000 in debt at the end of 1870, including $1,500 owed to players, and mismanagement by the early team officials was blamed for the shortfall, along with the fact some shareholders were in arrears. Still, the team had made $1,200 after July and "a fair dividend" was expected the following year.[22]

THE PHOENIX

IN 1871, FOR A $10 FEE, the team entered Harry Wright's newly formed National Association of Professional Base Ball Players, which enshrined the concept of professionalism and aimed to put an end to the type of messes that had marred the end of the previous season.[1] Along with the White Stockings, the NAPBBP had entries from Boston, Brooklyn, New York, Philadelphia, Troy, Cleveland, Fort Wayne, and Rockford.[2] The White Stockings, who could now count on a set schedule, moved to Lake Park, a new facility at Randolph Street and Michigan Avenue.[3] The enclosure had a seating capacity of seven thousand and a fan could secure season tickets for $15.[4]

Led by captain Jimmy Wood, who hit .378 for the year, the team was in first place in early October.[5] The club was showing signs of turning a large profit, with earnings of $20,000. By that point, the White Stockings were planning a $24,100 payroll for 1872, which would be a record.[6]

On October 8, 1871, Chicago awoke to two news items on the same page of the *Tribune*. A "terribly destructive conflagration" had started overnight, destroying buildings across twenty acres in the city's west division. "Thousands of citizens witness the grand but awful illumination," the paper reported. A couple of columns over, a large article documented the Chicago Base Ball Club's commanding lead in the championship race, with a 21-9 record compared to Philadelphia's 21-11 mark. The paper previewed the next day's game against Rockford, but another item mentioned that the fire,

This 1871 aerial view of Chicago in the October 21, 1871 issue of *Harper's Weekly* shows the team's Lake Park home grounds, to the viewer's left of the mouth of the Chicago River, where Millennium Park stands today. (Image courtesy of Brian Bernardoni)

still raging, was spreading northeast—in the direction of the White Stockings' ballpark, and so much else.[7]

The fire leveled Lake Park, leaving the team without a home, uniforms, equipment, and, more importantly, fans, who were busy reclaiming their lives from the smoldering ruins of the city. On October 14, the *Tribune* ran the most somber of headlines: "Everything." The subhead added "The Phantom City." Already, however, Chicago was "rising again," it said. In contrast, the paper reported in quite an understatement, "Up to Sunday night the dozen men who formed the White Stockings nine undoubtedly occupied a larger share of the public attention than any other body of private citizens in the city. By way of contrast, it may be said that they occupied very inferior positions in the attention of the people on Monday and Tuesday."[8]

THE GREAT CONFL

OCTOBER

The Business and Reside

Photographs show the devastation along Lake Park, home to the White Stockings, following the 1871 fire. (Library of Congress LC-USZC4-9440)

The site of the ballpark was a symbol of the new priorities in Chicago: The October 18 *Tribune* reported the old baseball grounds were now covered with wooded structures serving as temporary homes to several local businesses, just as water and gas service was slowly returning to some neighborhoods.[9] The team went away to play the last two weeks of the season at Union Grounds in Brooklyn, playing in uniforms borrowed from other teams and with little practice. New recruits for 1872 were released from their contracts, but the team hoped to stay together if it could win a championship and make some money in the process.[10] On October 30, they "suited up" against the Philadelphia Athletics in New York for a game that, it was said, would decide the championship: "Not two of the nine were dressed alike, all their uniforms having been consumed in the fire. They presented a most extraordinary appearance from the multi-colored nature of

their dress. All who could get white stockings did so, but they were not many.
… Where so much depends on the freedom of limb … their play to-day
with tight shirts, short pants, and hose in many cases a world too wide, was
indeed as creditable as it was surprising."[11] They lost 4–1. As was becoming
the norm, a high-level meeting would be required at season's end to sort the
final rankings out. At a meeting in early November, the association revised
clubs' records, denying a White Stockings request to "legalize" some of its
extra November contests on the road. Philadelphia was officially declared
the champion at 22-7, with Boston 22-10 and Chicago now only 20-9.[12]

Many of the business and civic leaders at the helm of the White Stockings
considered it folly to keep focusing on baseball in these trying times for
Chicago. The *Tribune* seemed to capture the team shareholders' sentiment
in its report on their November 11, 1871 meeting:

It would seem as though Chicago would, for next year, have enough on its hands in the care of its destitute and in the work of rebuilding, without any further dabbling in professional base ball. Even if it were possible—which it is not—to reconcile with our present position of alms-takers from the entire world the maintenance of an expensive professional club, we have no grounds on which to play games, and to fit grounds will cost four to five thousand dollars. The year 1872 will be a season for work in Chicago—hard, unceasing work for everybody, and we shall have little time to devote to an amusement, the enjoyment of which takes an entire afternoon. There will be no afternoons to spare, for some time to come, in Chicago. Baseball is a luxury which we can dispense with for at least one year, and there should be no further steps toward the reorganization of the White Stocking nine.[13]

Some White Stockings players fled east after the fire, but manager Tom Foley and several of his men stayed on, playing on a semiprofessional basis. For the next two years, however, attendance was dismal and play erratic.[14]

Spalding, in his memoirs decades later, would create a bit of confusion by listing Chicago as one of the league's entries for 1872 and 1873, but not listing them in results. Others since then, including Marshall Wright, established that neither the White Stockings nor any other Chicago team did compete in the NAPBBP for those two years, a fact confirmed in a brief 1876 retrospective of the sport in Chicago and various other articles.[15]

But organized baseball never fully went away in Chicago. The sentiment against continued activity among White Stockings management may have been prevalent, but it was not unanimous, as by the spring of 1872, a group involving the White Stockings' former president came together to start a new association, though not a club per se. For a week, they called themselves the Phoenix Base Ball Association, but soon reconsidered and settled on Chicago Base Ball Association. In an ironic contradiction to the *Tribune*'s editorial stance, they chose Sam J. Medill as their president, who was city editor of the newspaper and the brother of *Tribune* owner and then-Chicago Mayor Joseph Medill. The group aimed to raise $100,000.[16]

The main focus was on building a ballpark that could draw professional teams from other cities. In late May, teams from Baltimore and Cleveland came to Chicago to play before two thousand spectators at the new baseball grounds on the block bounded by 22nd, 23rd, Burnside, and Clark streets. The *Tribune* reporter, perhaps engaging in some brown-nosing with his boss, hailed the new facility as an improvement over Lake Park. With its fresh sod, Joliet gravel between the bases, small clubhouse, and grandstand and stands that added up to a capacity of 3,500, the paper said, "Better grounds or better accommodations could not have been met with in this or any other city." The ballpark was laid out to avoid direct sunlight in the eyes of pitchers and most fielders, and "the batter will strike in a southeasternly direction generally or across the wind, which is generally from the southwest in this windy town."[17]

Very few professional games would follow, and by the middle of 1873, the effort to retain some ties to professional baseball in the city had failed. The association, which held no regular lease on the grounds, only had $325 in its treasury. Medill left town to become the *Tribune*'s Washington correspondent in 1873. In July, a meeting was held to revive the old Chicago Base Ball Club, with one William Hulbert elected as an officer. Chicago would again have a professional team vying for the championship: "The reorganization of the Chicago Base Ball Club settles the future of the game in this city. The club is now in the hands of men of means, who will spare neither money nor time to carry out the original project of having in Chicago the best nine in the country."[18]

The *Tribune,* a few months after this pronouncement, wrote in April 1874 that "it may be doubted whether we shall ever see again the immense crowds, the strong interest and the hearty enthusiasm which used to attend the old White Stockings games." On May 13, the question seemed to be answered when a crowd estimated at five thousand to six thousand took in a 4–0 victory by the White Stockings over Philadelphia. The game's result, the *Tribune* wrote, "was accomplished notwithstanding the fact that the home club was outbatted and outfielded."[19]

The White Stockings did in fact fare badly over the season, finishing fifth with a losing record, 18½ games behind.[20] Attendance remained low, despite the steam-powered trains that facilitated the trip to the new 23rd Street Grounds.[21] The league itself was in disarray. Only more than half of 232 scheduled games were actually played.[22] Volunteer umpires failed to bring consistent rule enforcement and often made up rules—or ignored them—when faced with unfamiliar game situations.[23] As attendance decreased—in part because Boston continued to dominate easily every other team on its way to a 205-46 record from 1872 to 1875—player salaries declined, leading to an increase in the vicious cycle of gambling and game throwing, which further hurt the interest of games among regular spectators. Lack of success on the field and an economic downturn made it almost impossible for any team, save Boston, to meet its financial obligations.[24] The baseball world was headed for its second major reorganization in less than five years.

CHICAGO'S OWN LEAGUE

IN JUNE 1875, THE WHITE STOCKINGS' new owner William Hulbert scheduled "the biggest string of great games, ever attempted, by a single club in a month" and told his brother Eri that "I am bound to find out what they are made of."[1] The result was "some wonderful games, but on the whole not up to the standard."[2] The Chicagos finished the season sixth, in the middle of the pack. While it had been hoped the NAPBBP would infuse consistency in the schedule, things remained very lax, and yielded rankings that probably were not reflective of true strength. Boston was the undeniable winner in 1875 with a 71-8 record, good for a staggering .899 winning percentage. But behind them things were still as loopy as they had been in 1871. Hartford was second, posting .659 with a 54-28 record. At 53-20, Philadelphia was third with a far superior .726 winning percentage. Chicago was ranked seventh, with .448. The White Stockings were officially listed as being thirty-five games behind Boston, but they had only played sixty-nine games to Boston's eighty-two.[3]

Any way you cut it, the team had been mediocre. In fact, Hulbert knew as soon as he took the reins of the club early in the year that his players did not have what it took to win a pennant. The *New York Times* called them, before the season even began, "one of the best paid but most uncertain set of players in existence."[4] There was a great deal of pressure in the local press for the White Stockings to field a competitive nine; the *Chicago Tribune* called for management and Hulbert, whom it called "the great organizer of the game," to

William Hulbert was the early force behind the National League and its Chicago team. (Author's collection)

disband the team because "they are not what Chicago wants."[5] A member of the Chicago Board of Trade, Hulbert wanted to introduce business principles to baseball, which should be operated by owners and presidents, not the players themselves.[6] The lack of results provided him with an opening.

Hulbert hammered a deal that would force a reorganization of baseball and plant the seeds for a Chicago baseball dynasty. Before the season began, Hulbert, who had just been offered the club's presidency, had urged pitcher Albert G. Spalding—who had led the Boston Red Stockings to championships from 1872 to 1874 and would help them compile their pennant-winning 71-8 run in 1875—to come play in Chicago in 1876 and, so the rationalization went, restore competitive balance to the league.[7] If Spalding signed with Chicago, he was told, Hulbert would accept the board's offer to become president. In his memoir, Spalding recalled their conversation: "I told him that I was quite familiar with the entire situation; that it was the same all over the west—no city had any show under the present regime; that the spirit of gambling and graft held possession of the game everywhere; that the public was disgusted and wouldn't patronize the pastime, and, finally that unless there was a new deal throughout, with a cleaning out of the gamblers, both in and outside the Base ball profession, I, for one, proposed to quit."[8]

In June, Spalding signed a $2,000-a-year contract for the 1876 season (he would also receive a 25 percent share of gate receipts), along with the rest of Boston's "Big Four," who he had convinced to jump ship with him. This was no small get. Spalding was on his way to a 55-5 season in 1875, on the heels of a 52-16 record in 1874. He had won thirty-eight or more games for four straight years. Also coming home with Spalding was Ross Barnes, a second baseman who had gotten his start with the Forest Citys of Rockford in 1871. He had gone east with Spalding and had been the offensive standout on the perennial Boston championship team, batting .388 over five seasons. Barnes's average was helped by his skill at hitting "fair-foul" balls in the days before the ball had to at least stay fair past the bases.

There was one big obstacle. National Association rules forbade players to sign for another club before the end of their contract, and so the deal had to remain a secret.[9] Within a few weeks, however, the press broke the story about the secret contract, ensuring boos for the "Big Four" while they finished the season with Boston and then faced action against them by the National Association.[10] In the fall, in further violation of league bylaws, Spalding and Hulbert traveled to Philadelphia to sign Adrian Anson for $2,000, $200 more than he was making with the Athletics.[11]

Spalding and Anson went way back. Spalding, born in Byron, near Rockford, Illinois, was playing with Rockford's Forest Citys when they played an exhibition game against Anson's Marshalltown team in Iowa in the late 1860s.[12] Anson's personal story was a perfect illustration of Spalding's baseball-as-America narrative. According to his autobiography, Anson was born in 1852, the first white child to enter the world in Marshalltown,

Iowa, in the town's first log cabin, built by his father among "Indians of the Pottawattamie tribe, whose wigwams, or tepees, were scattered here and there upon the prairie and along the banks of the river."[13] His father was on Marshalltown's first baseball team, which Anson and his brother soon joined.

When the Forest Citys rolled through town, according to the Ansons, they brought three things with them: a delegation of "sporting men who had come prepared to wager their money," their own umpire, who "let Spalding pitch as many balls as he wished," and a potentially doctored ball. Spalding was supposedly so wild that Anson Sr. charged the mound and Spalding cowered and apologized. In 1871, as Spalding signed with the Boston Red Stockings, the Forest Citys recruited young Adrian Anson, when he led the team in fielding and batting while making $66 per month.[14]

Anson joined the Philadelphia Athletics in 1872 for $1,250 a year, while Spalding began his streak of pennants with Boston.[15] In 1874, Anson and Spalding traveled to England together as the Boston and Philadelphia squads went to show their wares across the Atlantic, Anson dubbing the two teams the "Argonauts of Base Ball."[16] Now, as Hulbert and Spalding conspired to assemble a championship team, they had included Anson in their flurry of illegal recruiting. Anson's numbers warranted the interest: he had put up Barnes-like stats without the fair-foul trick, batting .324 in 1875 after averaging .414, .398, and .331 in 1872, '73, and '74, respectively.[17]

Predictably, the eastern baseball establishment was preparing to expel the players in question from the league. Hulbert, fearful he would lose the nucleus of his new team, decided to create a league of his own. He told Spalding, "I have a new scheme. Let us anticipate the Eastern cusses and organize a new association before the March meeting of the league and see who will do the expelling."[18]

Spalding, who already saw himself as an executive, thought it was time to end what had been essentially a player-driven sport, and Hulbert readily agreed. Because of what he saw as "the irrepressible conflict between Capital and Labor," and a system in which only players seemed to make money, it seemed all too natural to him that a dedicated player, whose primary concern should be quality of play, leave management to his bosses.[19]

A few weeks later, the National League came a step further toward reality when Hulbert and officials from Cincinnati, Louisville, and St. Louis, all of whom had been shut out by the eastern clubs in league dealings, agreed on the principle of a new league. He then summoned the association's members to present them with the fait accompli. Years later, Spalding wrote that "this aggressive Base Ball magnate from the West, who had never been present at a similar meeting in his life" lectured them on "the evils of gambling that were threatening the very life of the game, reducing receipts, demoralizing players."[20]

There was little opposition when Hulbert produced a constitution for the National League of Professional Base Ball Clubs that listed as its goals to:

First—To encourage, foster and elevate the game of Base Ball.
Second—To enact and enforce proper rules for the exhibition and
   conduct of the game.
Third—To make baseball playing respectable and honorable.

Hulbert was also a firm believer that the game could enhance the patriotic and moral fiber of those who played and watched it. Instead of crowning himself president of the new league, Hulbert shrewdly nominated Morgan Bulkeley, of Hartford, Connecticut—who was later elected his state's governor—as its first leader, further co-opting the eastern clubs.[21]

The noble sentiments clashed with an already evident view of players as mere commodities, at least among the likes of Spalding. Before signing with Chicago, Anson had become engaged to be married in Philadelphia, and when his bride-to-be balked at a move west, he asked Hulbert and Spalding to release him from his contract over the winter of 1875–1876. After an initial refusal, Hulbert, whom Anson described after the fact to be "as honest as the day is long," was inclined to acquiesce but Spalding, of his own account, insisted they hold their ground, even in the face of Anson offering $1,000 for his freedom. Spalding knew Anson would never break his word and walk without their blessing. Anson arrived on the first day of training in street clothes still seemingly intent of talking his way out of Chicago, but Spalding was unbending. And so Anson became part of the White Stockings.[22]

Hulbert assumed the team presidency in December 1876. Earlier that year, in January, Hulbert had declared in a letter that "that bane of all sports, pool gambling has found an opening for its poisonous in the roots of the fraternity."[23] And so he soon expelled four Louisville players for throwing

William Hulbert's grave in Graceland Cemetery, just blocks from Wrigley Field, sports a modest, two-foot-high marker. More than one hundred years would go by before his induction into the Hall of Fame. (Photograph by author)

games. Open betting on league grounds was forbidden. Severe sanctions for violation of those rules were for the first time put in place, and contract jumping was—ironically, given the conditions surrounding the birth of the league—made an offense punishable by expulsion from the sport. Under the new provisions, liquor could not be sold at National League parks.[24]

Hulbert led the league until his death in Chicago in 1882. On his grave at Graceland Cemetery, a small monument was erected in the shape of a baseball and bears the names of the eight National League charter clubs: Boston, Chicago, Cincinnati, Hartford, Louisville, New York, Philadelphia, and St. Louis. After decades of efforts by former players, family members, and historians, Hulbert was elected to the baseball Hall of Fame by the Veterans Committee in 1995.

THE BIRTH OF A DYNASTY

FOR THE INAUGURAL YEAR of the National League, 1876, the White Stockings for the first time had the luxury of a clubhouse, located a block from their 23rd Street Grounds at 23rd and Wabash Avenue. Previous teams had been showering and suiting up at home. Now they could boast of a locker room "furnished in the most gorgeous style of the furniture dealer's art" in what the *Chicago Tribune* called a "fine mansion" at 1030 Wabash that even featured a billiards table in the basement. The club was financed through $20,000 in shares.[1]

The 1876 White Stockings, now managed by Spalding, who himself won forty-seven games (pitching in a staggering sixty of the White Stockings' sixty-six games), became the National League's first champions, six games ahead of St. Louis and Hartford. Barnes led the team with a league-best .429 batting average, followed by Anson (.356), 1875 returnee shortstop J. P. Peters (.351), and former Red Stocking first baseman Cal McVey (.347), who also pitched in the team's six non-Spalding games, winning five of them.[2] Hulbert had won the fight; his new players were in a class all their own and the game's image had been cleaned up. That's more than could be said about Hulbert's own image, at least in one newspaper's eye. The *Tribune* railed against him even as the team was wrapping the championship: "Mr. President Hulbert, while affable, is unsatisfactory, and any attempt to get an answer to a question from him about the future policy of the organization, of which he is the only visible head, is as fruitless as it would be to attempt to perceive a prominent bone in his well-fed body."[3] The *Evening Journal* described the city's sentiment toward the team itself: "They have won the coveted and Chicago is happy. Every man on the club has shown himself to be a gentleman as well as a ball player, and there has never been a breath of suspicion against them. They are a credit to the city of their adoption."[4] The *Inter Ocean* announced the following season's reshuffled lineup and predicted it would "comprise what is probably the strongest nine ever made up."[5] The *Tribune* had beaten everyone to the punch in mid-September, when it had declared the White Stockings champions with six games to go: "Enough is known and now announced to give good promise of the same success for 1877 that has attended the White Stockings of 1876."[6]

So much for premonitions. In 1877 Boston quickly reclaimed its place as the nation's premier ball club. Several Chicagos had subpar seasons—including Spalding, whose failing arm held him to just four games pitched. The team finished the season fifth out of six teams, more than fifteen games behind the despised Boston Red Stockings.[7]

Spalding ended his career at the end of the season to focus on managing the club and his budding sporting goods business.[8] Opened in March 1876 at 118 Randolph Street, Spalding's Baseball and Sporting Goods Emporium was benefitting from Spalding's connections to the game. He used them to secure a contract to provide all balls to the National League "to," he said, "insure uniformity and guard against fraud." He also was awarded the exclusive rights to publish the *Official League Book,* and quickly abused those rights when he launched his own *Spalding's Official Baseball Guide* and mentioned his contract with the league to make it seem like his guide too was official. When a new league president tried to stop the practice a few years later, it was too late: the name Spalding already was synonymous with baseball in Chicago and across the nation.[9]

Eager to boost attendance, the team returned to its pre-fire location in 1878 with the new Lakefront Park on the downtown lakefront at Randolph and Michigan, on a converted former dump, where Millennium Park sits today. The venue was a godsend for Hulbert and Spalding; only a two-minute walk now separated businessmen from their team.[10] Better yet, the site was a bargain. It had been deeded to the city by the federal government, with the understanding that it not be sold or used for profit.[11] But profit was made. The White Stockings netted $11,827 in 1877, helped by the fact they

J. S. Thompson & Co. Printers. Times Building, 88 Fifth Avenue, Chicago.

Led by Al Spalding, the White Stockings won the inaugural National League title in 1876. (Digital restoration by author of poster from Chicago History Museum collection, ICHi-51406)

rented the grounds for only $5,000. The team earned between $23,000 and $32,000 during the 1878, 1879, and 1881 seasons, at a time when season tickets could be had for $5.[12] At the beginning of the 1881 season, the club had $6,764.74 on hand.[13] For the period from September 1876 to December 1877, Hulbert and Spalding each received a salary of $2,500. Anson was paid $2,200. Total payroll exceeded $21,000.[14] This in spite of lackluster play by the Whites, who were now led by Anson as captain— the only holdover from the 1876 squad[15]—and managed by shortstop Bob Ferguson.[16] To add revenue and to burnish his own income, Anson managed a skating park on the field in the winter. Ladies and children could skate for $3, men for $4, and couples for $5.[17]

Chicago finished fourth in '78 and '79, but there were signs of hope. The club could have contended in 1879 had it not been for a kidney infection

Opened in 1878 and grandiosely refurbished over the 1882–1883 off season, Lakefront Park was deemed the finest in the world by *Harper's Weekly*. The team was expelled from the location after the '84 season when it was "discovered" that the ballpark, located at the southeast corner of Randolph and Michigan, was a for-profit venture on public land. (Author's collection)

that sidelined Anson, who still batted .396, and a line drive to the head that reduced pitching sensation Terry Larkin (31-23, 2.44 ERA) to a suicide-shortened life of mental illness.[18]

To avoid team jumping, the league instituted the reserve clause that winter, ensuring that Chicago would be able retain its nucleus of quality players for the foreseeable future. In 1880, four of the starting nine batted better than .300, and centerfielder George Gore led the league with a .360 average. The team enjoyed pitching not seen since the days of Spalding, with Larry Corcoran winning 43 and losing 14 and Fred Goldsmith posting a 21-3 record. Corcoran lead the league with 268 strikeouts and recorded the first of his three no hitters between 1880 and 1884. By season's end, the team

Spalding assembled the best team of the early 1880s, which went on to be one of baseball's most enduring powerhouses for more than ten years. Adrian Anson, George Gore, and King Kelly took turns leading the team in batting throughout the decade, and they combined for five league batting champion titles over the period. Ned Williamson and Abner Dalrymple added power and were crowned the league's home run champion in 1884 and 1885, respectively. On the mound, Larry Corcoran won thirty-plus games every year from 1880 through 1885, and Fred Goldsmith added at least twenty wins a season over the 1880–1883 stretch. The team would win five NL pennants between 1880 and 1889, but would lose the championship of the world to Charles Comiskey's St. Louis Browns. Over a twelve-year stretch beginning in 1880, the White Stockings would only finish worse than third once. (Author's collection)

claimed its second pennant, and the first since 1876, beating second-place Providence by a staggering fifteen games.[19] Reminiscing years later, catcher Mike Kelly dubbed the 1880 White Stockings team the best of all time.[20] They clinched on September 15 with ten games to go, and for once, the *Tribune* said, it was "beyond doubt or controversy. . . . The team has been banded together with consummate ability by Capt. Anson. . . . [I]t may well be doubted if any one ball-player has made so conspicuous a figure on the diamond field as Anson has done."[21]

After the 1880 season, the team played an exhibition game against Buffalo that received a good deal of advance publicity because it was to feature two experiments: one with a square bat model championed by Harry Wright, the other with "a new style of ball, the peculiarity of which is the presence in the centre of a small globe of cork." The flat bat was deemed a "flat failure" because any hit not made with the center of the thing "turned the bat in the player's hands, causing a disagreeable sting in the palms." The squads went back to the round variety to finish the game and truly gauge what the ball prototype had to offer. It too was deemed "unsatisfactory" because "the ball didn't sound natural when hit by the bat and, though it went very swift and far when fairly hit, it behaved awkwardly when batted on the ground." Hulbert and the players strongly opposed the adoption of either technology.[22]

In 1881, the team did just fine with the old-fashioned bat and ball and repeated as champion, with Anson batting .399 and leading the league in hits (137) and runs batted in (eighty-two). Leftfielder Abner Darlymple remained in top form, hitting .323 on the heels of a .330 season. Sophomore Kelly improved to the same mark of .323. Corcoran led the league with thirty-one wins and Goldsmith added twenty-four victories.[23]

As far as the *New York Times* was concerned, all of this would become a footnote in history about a soon-to-be forgotten sport, which was dangerous, overly complicated, and corrupted by gambling. The paper predicted in August 1881, "There is really reason to believe that baseball is gradually dying out in this country. . . . Probably the time is now ripe for the revival of cricket." Statistics cited by the paper to emphasize how the game, with the introduction of harder balls, had become more hazardous "than to fill lighted kerosene lamps," actually reveal the popular enthusiasm for the game: Given the number of baseball-related injuries, one can only conclude the game had spread like wildfire through the population. According to the paper, over the previous decade, there had been exactly 37,518 accidents stemming from the game, "of which 3 percent have been fatal; 25,611 fingers and 11,016 legs were broken during the decade in question, while 1,900 eyes were permanently put out and 1,648 ribs were fractured." The *Times* deadpanned, "Had not the popularity of the game begun to decline some two years ago, it would undoubtedly have been demanded by Western Democrats that base-ball cripples should be pensioned by the Government, a measure which would at once bankrupt our National Treasury."[24]

Nobody must have briefed the Chicago nine, or their fans, on he fact baseball was dying. With their lineup virtually unchanged, the White Stockings clinched a record third-straight pennant in 1882. Chicago squeezed past Providence by three games, down from nine the previous year, after a mad chase that captured the city's imagination. In fifth place in the middle of June, the White Stockings slowly caught up to Providence and finally squeezed past them with three straight wins against them in a September series. "For Chicago to have won the emblem of supremacy under such conditions is by all odds the most creditable achievement in the annals of ball playing," the *Tribune* boasted.[25]

Though it sat atop the rankings at the end of the regular schedule, Chicago had agreed to play nine exhibition games against Providence after the season. Controversy ensued when some in Providence dubbed the matches a "championship series," eliciting what one newsman said was visible "disgust" in Spalding.[26] After Providence humiliated the new champions in a three-game sweep in Providence, with the aggregate score of 19–9, the Chicago papers declared that "nobody cares" and that "Chicagoans "take no stock in exhibition games." Chicago tied things up by going 4-1 over the next contests in New York and Chicago, where crowds averaged only one thousand. The Whites put Providence away in the last game in Fort Wayne 19–7, but there was no boasting from the *Tribune,* which called the game "a great disappointment . . . as the players seemed to take no interest in it."[27]

The players could be forgiven for being somewhat weary, as Spalding could never seem to leave well enough alone. After the lackluster Providence series, the club came back to Chicago for a "benefit" game . . . for themselves. It was noteworthy because Spalding took to the mound for the first time in years to lead a squad that also featured Gore, Darlymple, Pfeffer, and Williamson against a squad on which Anson was supplemented by Kelly, Corcoran, and Goldsmith. Spalding, whom the paper said remained "the prince of straight-arm pitchers," was pegged for four earned runs to Goldsmith's one, but the Spaldings won 10–6. The 1,200 spectators were also treated to a variety of skills battles, which demonstrated Williamson's awesome prowess, lest anyone think 1880s players were not true athletes: He bagged the base-running contest with a 14.5-second performance, won the 100-yard dash in 10.75 seconds, and propelled the ball farther than anyone with back-to-back 390-foot throws. The "benefit" netted $50 to $75 for each player.[28]

Not that they should have needed the extra revenue. The team made enough money with its three straight pennants for Spalding, the new president and owner after Hulbert's death, to turn Lakefront Park into a venue of grandiose amenities.

After the team drew 111,452 spectators, or 2,796 per game in 1882, *Harper's Weekly* reported that "with this fine patronage, made up in good part of the finer classes of the community, the Chicago Club is amply able to maintain its costly team of players, and to equip its grounds and fixtures." Indeed, Spalding spent $10,000 on improving the ballpark. The team had enough cash to spend $1,800 on paint alone. The remodeled grandstand could seat two thousand, and there were six thousand additional seats in the bleachers along the foul lines. All told, Lakefront Park could now accommodate ten thousand spectators, with the lowest seats six feet above ground to allow for a better view of the game. A pagoda was home to the First Cavalry Band. From his telephone-equipped luxury box atop the grandstand—one of eighteen he had built—Spalding commandeered the crew of forty-one employees required each game day to operate the grounds. *Harper's* declared the ballpark "indisputably the finest in the world in respect of seating accommodations and conveniences" that, compared to other ballparks, "might be termed palatial." The magazine estimated the team's total expenses for players, employees, travel, and ballpark at $60,000 for the season and concluded, "the fact that so large an outlay can be safely made tells its own story on the popularity of base-ball."[29]

The heavy investment and unbridled optimism could not prevent a slightly disappointing season in 1883. Only Gore and Anson hit above .300 and Goldsmith slumped a bit (25-19) while Corcoran maintained a

The 1880–1881–1882 championship run by the White Stockings was the high point of Cap Anson's storied career. So strong was his mark on the White Stockings that the franchise became known as Anson's Colts. He batted .331 over twenty-two seasons, the last nineteen of them as player-manager. Anson still holds Cubs franchise career records in runs (1,719), hits (3,055), doubles (528), and RBIs (1,879). His 1887 batting average of .421 is still the highest-ever for a player on Chicago's NL franchise. His overt racism remains a blot on his achievements. (Author's collection)

.630 winning percentage.[30] Though overall attendance rose to 126,376, the game-day average was down to 2,477 as the White Stockings finished four games behind Boston.[31] The foursome of Anson at first base, Fred Pfeffer at second, Ed Williamson at short, and Toms Burns at third played for the first time together that year, and became known as the "stonewall" infield for its supposed ability to gobble-up grounders and spare line drives.[32] As in the case of another Cubs infield later, it was mostly hype. From 1883 through 1889, the White Stockings had an average NL fielding rank of fifth, and finished better than fourth only once (second in 1888).

The 1884 finish was no better than in '83, though a late-season surge and some strong individual performances offered reason for hope. The White Stockings finished twenty-two games behind Providence, but they tied for fourth with the New York Gothams, who they caught thanks to a monstrous four-game sweep in early October during which they outscored New York 51–17. Newcomer pitcher John Clarkson (10-3) stepped in as the team's second ace behind Corcoran (35-23), as Goldsmith faded (9-11). Mike Kelly had a banner year, hitting .354 and scoring 120 runs, and Ned Williamson was National League home run champion with 27.[33]

The team could not translate its 180-foot left field and 196-foot right field into another pennant in spite of a gift by the league. Chicago had consistently led the league in ground-rule doubles and, when those were declared home runs by the National League for the 1884 season, the team was credited with 142 home runs, almost five times the previous league record . . . this after hitting just thirteen home runs in 1883. Four White Stockings hit more than twenty home runs, when no other player in the league slugged more than fourteen. As historian Michael Benson concluded, the team's skills had not changed radically, the rules had.[34] Another piece of evidence that there was in fact nothing new and exciting at the ballpark was attendance, which went into a free fall, as only 88,218 attended the team's fifty-seven home games, for an average of just 1,547 a game.[35] To make matters worse, the team was forced to look for new grounds. In June 1884, the U.S. government secured an injunction to keep the team from playing at Lakefront Park after the season because Spalding's outfit was declared, belatedly, a commercial venture. Spalding's heavy investment had been largely wasted, and plans were made for a new ballpark.[36]

KEEPING THE
STOCKINGS WHITE

IN JULY 1884, Spalding had his secretary write to the Toledo ball club in preparation for a game. The purpose what to remind Toledo that it had agreed to keep Moses Fleetwood Walker, its black catcher, off the diamond for the game.[1] Spalding claimed to be acting under pressure from his players, which would have been highly unusual.

Some months earlier, the White Stockings had been prepared to take the field against Toledo when Anson took notice of Walker and deadpanned: "Get that nigger off the field."[2] When its opponents refused to play without their catcher, Chicago agreed to play to avoid losing its share of the gate.[3] But on several other occasions Anson had his way.[4] In 1887, Anson successfully kept the Newark Little Giants from lining up with Walker and black pitcher George Stovey by refusing to have his team take to the field if they played.[5] That same year, Anson worked with other baseball powers to prevent John Montgomery Ward, owner of the New York Giants, from promoting Stovey to the major leagues, and the owners established the "Gentleman's Agreement" to segregate athletes.[6] By 1895, the number of blacks playing professional baseball had dwindled from twenty to none.[7]

About the time it was relentlessly suppressing black players, White Stockings' management secured the services of a black boy, Clarence Duval, as the club's new mascot to provide entertainment to their fans and themselves during lazy afternoons at the park. Duval also doubled as a good-luck charm,

The White Stockings' black mascot Clarence Duval was both a good-luck charm and a target of abuse by players and management. (Author's collection)

whose head had to be rubbed when the team was in trouble on the field. Duval was constantly referred to, both in the press and by Anson, as "Pickaninny, nig, coon, or darkey mascot." So mistreated was the boy that he ran away to Omaha, only to be "reclaimed" by the team during a road trip.[8]

Anson and Spalding's attitude was part of an institutionalized nationwide movement to rescind some of the post–Civil War advances in the treatment of blacks. In 1883, as Anson openly displayed his racism, the Supreme Court struck down the 1875 Civil Rights Act, which guaranteed blacks equal access to public facilities such as ballparks, on the basis that the federal government could not regulate private relationships and behavior. The "separate-but-equal" provisions that spread throughout the country would be upheld in 1896 in the U.S. Supreme Court's *Plessy v. Ferguson* ruling.[9]

Several dozen black players performed at the major and minor league levels through the end of the nineteenth century, overcoming the daunting obstacles put in place by the baseball establishment as well as rampant racism.[10] In 1867 black clubs, most prominently in the East, played against each other in a championship format. That December, however, the National

Association of Base Ball Players voted to deny a petition for membership by a Philadelphia club and unanimously adopted a policy "against the admission of any club that may be composed of one or more colored persons."[11] In 1871, the new National Association of Professional Base Ball Players did not include a clause against black players in its constitution, but that would not remove discrimination from the highest levels of the game.[12] Some 1880s and 1890s players with ambiguous features were rumored to be black and their playing days were shortened as a result.[13]

"Fleet" Walker and his brother Welday broke into the majors in 1884 with the Toledo franchise of the short-lived American Association. Fleet, a catcher, hit .251 in fifty-four games that year. He was frequently hurt; catchers did not wear protective equipment then, but one of his pitchers, Tony Mullane, also did his part: "[Walker] was the best catcher I ever worked with, but I disliked a Negro and whenever I had to pitch to him I used to pitch anything I wanted without looking at his signals," resulting in a number of unwarranted injuries.[14] The *Sporting News* was understated in its description of the life for the rare black players on professional teams: "Race prejudice exists in professional baseball ranks to a marked degree, and the unfortunate son of Africa who makes his living as a member of a team of white professionals has a rocky road to travel."[15] The hatred by white teammates was so intense—one player declared he would rather have his "heart cut out" rather than being photographed with a black teammate—that many black players exited professional ball quickly.[16]

Black players realized that success lay in taking a parallel path. In 1885, the first salaried all-black team was organized in New York.[17] By the turn of the century, "Negro" baseball was very active in Chicago.[18] Even then, the best black players earned less than $500 per season, which was less than the average white minor leaguer and four times less than the major-league average.[19] In the first decade of the twentieth century, the Leland Giants would become Chicago's black baseball powerhouse. The team was led by Andrew "Rube" Foster, a screwball pitcher from Texas, and played in Auburn Park (79th and Wentworth) before showing its wares at 69th and Halsted and, in 1910, at 6221 S. Halsted. It was the first all-black team in the city to be able to obtain a fifty-fifty split of gate receipts when it played against white teams. In 1911, the team would move into Old Roman's Park, at 39th and Wentworth, after it was vacated by Charles Comiskey's White Sox.[20]

Like William Hulbert before him, Foster would use Chicago as the launching pad for a league. He joined the Chicago Union Giants in 1902 for $40 a month, and stayed for one season. In 1908, Foster returned to Chicago to manage the Leland Giants. In 1910, he started his own club with several Leland Giants, eventually naming the team the Chicago American Giants. Confident in the ability of established baseball to empower and affirm the identity of African American communities, Foster started work in Chicago toward the Negro National League. In 1916, his American Giants were denied entry into the semipro and amateur Chicago City League because they were a professional outfit. That fall, they would beat the white Magnets, who had just won the City League. By 1920, Foster's Negro National League would be a reality, and he was the first president of the first permanent African American league, with Chicago as its heart. In addition to continuing to run the American Giants, Foster received 5 percent of the league's gate receipts.[21] But the efforts of Spalding and other baseball "pioneers" to keep the major leagues white had succeeded to keep black talent and fans in the shadows, where they would remain until Branch Rickey and Jackie Robinson brought African Americans back to the big leagues in 1947.

WEST SIDE HOME

IN JUNE 1885, the new grounds were ready for the White Stockings' first game. Spalding was leasing land that had been appraised at $750,000. The $30,000 structure, called West Side Park, was bounded by Loomis to the west, Throop to the east, Harrison to the south, and Congress to the north. The u-shaped grandstand was a wooden structure, but a $10,000 brick wall had been erected around the park, creating, the *Mirror of American Sports* said, "without doubt the finest [ballpark] in America, and [. . .] probably not surpassed by any athletic grounds in the world." The grandstand counted 2,500 numbered seats. The team offered private boxes, labeled A through L, located above the grandstand. There were an additional three thousand open seats, and the left and right field walls could be lined with temporary bleachers.[1]

The city's public transportation network was improving. Chicago was in the midst of a boom in streetcar construction—from eighty miles of track in 1880, the number expanded to 119 miles in 1885. By 1890, Chicago boasted 193 miles of streets equipped with rails, the third highest total in the nation behind Philadelphia and Boston.[2] The field could be reached by streetcars on Madison, Van Buren, and Harrison streets. Although not as convenient as the team's previous location on the lakefront, fans could still reach Congress Street Park in fifteen minutes from downtown.[3] Whereas the early amateur teams that played on the city's west side in the 1860s found themselves "out on these prairies,"[4] the neighborhood was now home to only three small green expanses other than the ballpark: Union Park, which expanded

The White Stockings' 1885 new West Side Park at Congress and Throop. (Author's collection)

on fourteen acres; Jefferson Park, with five acres; and Vernon Park, which spanned four acres.[5]

One of the new park's more remarkable features exemplified the team's dedication to middle- and upper-class values: center field was reserved for carriage cars. Well-to-do Chicagoans could be driven to the edge of the bicycle track that surrounded the grass and watch games from their parked vehicles.[6] In the face of the eyebrow-raising hobbies of some immigrant groups, including Germans (who practiced gymnastics but went beer-drinking afterward), baseball had come in the 1860s to embody and defend the ideals of "Victorian Americans."[7] Organized baseball might have allowed working-class players on its professional teams—by the early 1880s, more than one-third of retired major leaguers were occupied as blue-collar workers and nearly one-half as low white collar[8]—but the game remained torn between its early image as the gentleman's game and that of a truly American, national pastime accessible to all. Like the early republic, baseball officials were not easily able to reconcile their democratic aspirations with their middle- and upper-class roots. Glossing over the game's glaring racial exclusion, Spalding, who succeeded Hulbert as team president after his death in 1882, proclaimed that "the genius of our institutions is democratic; Base Ball is a democratic game. . . . We are a cosmopolitan people, knowing no arbitrary class distinctions, acknowledging none." Yet, when praising baseball's ability to advance social mobility, he focused only on "the brilliant array of statesmen, judges, lawyers, preachers, teachers, engineers, physicians, surgeons, merchants, manufacturers, men of eminence in all the professions and in every avenue of commercial activity, who have graduated from the ball field to enter upon honorable careers as American citizens of the highest type, each with a sane mind in a sound body."[9]

The club found itself in a setting fitting such lofty aspirations. The park's "locality [was] a favorite residence district and brick and stone dwellings of a superior class overlook the grounds on every side."[10] The Congress Street grounds stood in the eleventh ward, home to Mayor Carter Harrison Sr.[11] and was described as "a residence section of the middle class, pretty evenly populated by native people mostly living in their own homes."[12]

Just beyond was a potential fan base that, for now, remained untapped. To the east—across the street—began the city's nineteenth ward, which the Census Office described in 1890 as largely Irish with strong German and Bohemian contingents. Poles and Italians lived in the ward's eastern section. "The population was chiefly of laborers and the working classes, employes [sic] of the large factories, sugar refineries, glucose works, and warehouses of the ward and vicinity. There was also a large vicious element of both sexes. Aside from the industrial premises the ward was occupied by cheap boarding and lodging houses and hotels, dwellings and residences improving in grade toward the west end."[13]

A few blocks away to the northeast was the eighteenth ward, most of which was dubbed "a 'slum' region" where unsanitary and unsavory conditions prevailed. The western edge of the ward, closest to the park, was "a residence district with a native population, improving in quality to the west line, where the character of the dwellings and occupants merged into that of ward 11."[14]

Meanwhile, Cap Anson found a new symbol of the team's wholesomeness. Anson's abuse of the black team mascot Clarence Duval was in marked contrast with the treatment received by Willie Hahn, the six-year-old son of a hat wholesaler who lived on Throop Street, across the street from the team's new ballpark. Young Willie's favorite playground had been the vegetable patches that were replaced by the infield and grandstand. Instead of watching after tomatoes, he began attending the White Stockings' practices and was adopted as the team mascot. Willie was entrusted with the keys to the clubhouse, became third baseman Ned Williamson's personal batboy, and artists painted his portrait.[15]

By late summer, the White Stockings were neck and neck with the New York Giants in their hunt to rekindle the glory years of the early 1880s, and Chicago had pennant fever. On September 29, 1885, the team played New York before ten thousand spectators at West Side Park. The captains agreed the overflow crowd was so large it would be hard to field balls, and so balls hit into the crowd would be good for three bases. Before the game, a full marching band led both teams in a parade through the grounds in front of the president of the league, representatives of several major league teams, and Mayor Harrison. In New York, crowds "as dense as they had been during the intense excitement of the last election" gathered around downtown tickers. The White Stockings won 7–4. Attesting to the size of the crowd and the players' aiming abilities, the home team hit twenty-six triples (eleven were King Kelly's) and New York seven. The *Chicago Tribune* described the White Stockings as having played "the more brainy game, depending for victory as much upon their heads as upon their arms and legs."[16] To the *Chicago Daily Inter Ocean,* "it seemed as if the home team were giants and the New Yorks were pygmies" in "as carefully played a game as has ever been played in this city. . . . The shouts could be heard a mile." In New York, the paper reported, "no one had a word to say, but it was evident that some fond hopes had been suddenly blasted."[17] The next day, eleven thousand gathered to see Chicago beat the Giants 2 to 1 in "another Waterloo" that secured the pennant for Chicago by two games and ensured, according to the *Inter-Ocean,* that "Gotham Grieves."[18]

The turnaround from 1884 was dramatic. The eight starting position players who won the 1885 National League title were the very same who had finished twenty-two games out of first place the year before. There were two reasons. As Corcoran's arm died—fifty-nine starts for thirty-five wins in '84, seven starts and five wins in '85—Clarkson carried the team on his shoulders: seventy starts (62 percent of the team's games), fifty-three wins (61 percent of Chicago's victories), an ERA of 1.85, and a league-leading 308 strikeouts. Pitching sensation Jim McCormick, added late in the season, compiled a .833 winning percentage, going 20-4.[19]

And the field players got their act together on defense. The team of the mid-1880s included the "stonewall infield," so proclaimed by Anson and some sportswriters. Made up of Anson at first, Pfeffer at second, Williamson at third, and Burns at shortstop, it first came together in 1883 and continued through 1889. Like Tinker, Evers, and Chance later, the infield's actual claim on the moniker was probably tenuous: The team's overall average fielding rank over those years was fifth. After ranking eighth in the league fielding average in '84 to go along their number-one rank in every offensive category, the White Stockings corrected course in '85, finishing fourth in fielding and regaining a bit of their tenuous claim to their "stonewall infield" nickname, while staying on top of most offensive categories. The statistics spoke for themselves. Kelly scored 124 runs to go along an uncharacteristically "low" .288 batting average. Anson batted .310 and Gore had another "routine" year with .313.[20]

The Chicago fans—who had found their way back to the ballpark (attendance for the year was 119,318, or 2,057 spectators per game)—had been an effective tenth man, to the point that someone wrote a letter to the editor in the *New York Sun* "remembering the terrifying influence of Chicago's crowds upon umpires."[21] There had been heavy betting on the series, the *Inter Ocean* admonishing "it is very wrong to bet, especially against the Chicago nine."[22] The throngs of New Yorkers who came to Chicago did not heed the advice and bet heavily on their team. Anson said "there was not a man on the delegation that accompanied the Giants that did not lose, and lose heavily on the games, which went a long way toward illustrating the glorious uncertainties of baseball."[23]

Disgruntled gamblers made allegations of game fixing by Chicago, New York, Providence, Boston, and Philadelphia throughout the season, but Spalding and the New York management emphatically denied it.[24]

For the meaningless last game of the series, another ten thousand spectators showed up on the West Side in spite of "one of the most disagreeable

A Massachusetts minor league sensation signed by the White Stockings at age twenty-one, John Clarkson compiled a 137-57 record over just four years with the team. In 1885, he nearly matched the team's pennant-clinching .777 winning percentage, posting a 53-16 record (.768) with a 1.85 ERA and pitching sixty-eight complete games. Shown here in an 1887 baseball card, he would become part of Spalding's wholesale liquidation after that season, but would post just one losing season over the remaining eight years of his career. (Library of Congress LC-DIG-bbc-0110F)

CLARKSON, P. Chicago.

COPYRIGHTED BY GOODWIN & CO. 1887.

days on record for baseball playing." Before the first inning, the two teams met at home plate, where a large "1885" had been inscribed. New York's captain, John Montgomery Ward, then gave a speech: "Captain Anson, we came to Chicago hoping and expecting to win this last series of games. But you have beaten us fairly and by good ball-playing, and therefore we have no complaints. On the contrary, as a souvenir of the season's struggle and as an earnest of our friendly feeling, the New York Club presents to the Chicago Club this flag." He handed Anson a large silk pennant that read,

Team mascot Willie Hahn paraded with the 1885 gold-lettered pennant gifted by New York. (Author's collection)

"New York to Chicago, 1885" in gold letters. Cap answered, "Our pleasure in any victory is tempered by regret that we should have won against such a generous foe." Mascot Willie Hahn then paraded the flag as the two teams joined in "Auld Lang Syne." New York won 10–8 but, no matter, the crowd was dancing jigs in the stands between innings. It had been fourteen years almost to the day since the Chicago Fire had helped deny Chicago its first pennant.[25] But the hardest was yet to come, as another foe lurked.

THE NATIONAL LEAGUE
AIN'T THE WORLD

GONE WERE THE DAYS WHEN WINNING a pennant meant a team could go home as champions. For now, the White Stockings could only claim the title of 1885 National League Champions. They would have to defeat the St. Louis Browns before they could call themselves "Champions of the World." In 1881, in response to Hulbert's decision to ban liquor from National League parks and the league's stance against Sunday baseball, a group of brewers had organized the American Association to sell more beer.[1] Dubbed the Beer Ball League, the group was formally born in Cincinnati, a city that Hulbert had banned from the National League for violating its liquor and Sunday rules. Though there was no American Association team in Chicago, St. Louis soon emerged as a strong regional rival. The league gained early success by charging only twenty-five cents for seats, half the average National League price. Unbound by the reserve clause, association clubs raided their National rivals' rosters during the 1882–1883 offseason. Pressured into a corner, the National League agreed to recognize the American Association as a major league, the latter agreeing in exchange to enter the reserve-clause system. The deal was enshrined in the National Agreement, which set salary limits at $2,000.[2] By late 1883, St. Louis was making profits of between $50,000 and $70,000 and all but one of its fellow America Association members were in the black.[3]

In 1885, the Browns were led by Charles Comiskey, the son of a Chicago alderman. Born on the West Side in 1859 and a former member of its Libertys amateur team, he had joined the Browns in 1882 and had just become their captain-manager.[4] With him at the helm, the St. Louis Browns dominated the association and won the pennant. Continuing a tradition begun the year before by the champions of each league, the Browns challenged the White Stockings to a championship series. They agreed on a twelve-game playoff format, with games held in each city, plus Pittsburgh, Cincinnati, Baltimore, Philadelphia, and Brooklyn. The series ended after just six games over a dispute not dissimilar to a schoolyard spat. In St. Louis's eyes, the score was 3–2 in the Browns' favor, as one game had been cut short by rowdy St. Louis fans, and the Browns considered the contest discounted. Spalding argued he had never agreed to discount the game's result and considered the game a forfeit, which made the series a 3-3 tie. Moreover, because the games had been played in St. Louis, Spalding argued the result was meaningless because the series had taken place "upon their grounds and under the authority of their umpires."[5]

The Chicago newspapers proved better sports than Spalding, announcing that the Whites had lost the title of "Champions of the World" to the Browns.[6] An arbitration board eventually ended the controversy by declaring a tie and dividing the $1,000 purse equally among the two teams.[7]

Fittingly, the debate would be put to rest once and for all the following October, on the playing field. The White Stockings returned the very same team in 1886, the only major change being the addition of pitcher Jocko Flynn. New York failed to provide opposition to Chicago during the unprecedented 124-game schedule. Instead, it was Detroit that threatened to deny the Whites their second straight pennant. Chicago hung on and won the National League title by two and a half games. The pitching staff of Clarkson, Jim McCormick, and Flynn combined for a 90-34 record and an ERA of less than 2.50. Anson batted .374 but was bested for the team lead by Kelly, who had been demoted to the role of utility player. Jimmy Ryan had shown promise the previous year and was given Kelly's right field job after Kelly's lowly .288 in '85. But Kelly appeared in 118 games and batted .388, with a team-high 155 runs, claiming the batting title, as he had in 1884.[8] The team shattered its attendance record with 142,438 for the year, but the per-game average of 2,297 fans was still shy of the 1882 figure.[9]

On the other side of the Mississippi River, the Browns also repeated, setting the stage for a rematch in the "Championship of the World" series. A more

CHAPTER 9

RIVAL BASE-BALL CAPTAINS RENEWING THEIR YOUTH.
Capt. Anson—"You dassent!"   Capt. A.—"Yah!"
Capt. Comiskey—"Yes, I dast!"   Capt. C.—"Yah!"

In 1890, Charles Comiskey (left) was player-manager of the Players' League's Chicago Pirates. Though the Pirates and White Stockings did not face each other on the field, this 1890 cartoon looks back at Comiskey's old rivalry with Anson, and unknowingly previews the Cubs-Sox rivalry of the twentieth century. (Author's collection)

standard format was agreed upon, with three games to be played in each city. After taking two out of the first three games, the White Stockings dropped the series 4 to 2. Although he conceded that his team had been "fairly beaten," Anson whined just like Spalding had done a year before: "But had some of the players taken as good a care of themselves prior to these games as they

RYAN.—CENTRE FIELD.
SMOKE AND CHEW
"YUM YUM" TOBACCO.
A. BECK & CO., CHICAGO, ILL.

Jimmy Ryan led the NL in 1888 with 182 hits and sixteen home runs and is the only Cub to hit for the cycle twice. He averaged .311 over an eighteen-year career that, save for its last two years with the Washington Senators in 1902–1903, was spent entirely in Chicago—fifteen seasons with the White Stockings, Colts, and Cubs and one with the Players' League in 1890. Though he remains in the Cubs' top ten all-time in every hitting category except home runs, he never found his way to Cooperstown. (Library of Congress LC-DIG-bbc-0566F)

were in the habit of doing when the League season was in full swing, I am inclined to believe that there might have been a different tale to tell."[10]

The shaken dominance of the National League exemplified that "baseball can be said to know no North, no South, no East, no West," as Spalding had declared in that year's guide. The game was even spreading to Ontario.[11]

THE SABBATH BATTLES

ON GAME DAY, FEW BLUE-COLLAR WORKERS or unsavory characters so feared by Spalding were to be found at the ballpark. Sunday games had been forbidden by the National League in 1878—only a few exhibition games took place on the Sabbath before then—thus precluding workers, whose only day off was Sunday, from attending the games. Immigrants—German and Irish being the most numerous—made up three-fifths of the city's population. They celebrated Sundays as a day for leisurely activities and beer gardens.[1] Yet, though it was for some of them a stone's throw away from their home, the Whites' park was closed on their holiday and, in any event, no beer could be purchased there.[2]

In 1880, Cincinnati's ballpark was open on Sundays, and served beer. At the end of the season, the NL met to formally vote against both practices, and when Cincinnati voted "no," it was expelled. The *Chicago Tribune*'s parody of Cincinnati's executives reflected the prevalent bias against opening the game to the masses: "We cannot maintain a ball team in Cincinnati unless we are permitted to lower the tone of baseball to the level of beer-guzzlers and Sabbath breakers. The respectable people of Cincinnati will not patronize the game and we are reduced to the necessity of catering to the patronage of the loafer and bummer elements."[3]

In 1887, Spalding came to the defense of Sunday entertainment, but stuck to his guns on Sunday pro baseball. Sunday activities were coming under increasing fire in the state legislature, but Spalding argued that Sabbath rules precluded amateur baseball from helping forge the strong moral fiber of young blue-collar men.[4]

Spalding's attitude was different when it came to staging professional games on the Sabbath. In his memoirs, writing about rival leagues that allowed Sunday play, he argued that "unrestricted Sunday games in violation of law and the wide-open liquor traffic could not but be prejudicial."[5] A typical mix of moral and financial considerations—Sunday baseball represented enormous potential gate receipts—had him come to favor Sunday games, with the implication that it applied to respectable clubs (the National League or its recently organized minor league clubs) and that liquor continued to be absent from the parks. Recalling having been "importuned, almost with tears, to ignore the law," and preferring to forego a hefty game purse rather than play a Sunday exhibition game, Spalding described his position on the issue:

> I am not, nor have I ever been, opposed to Sunday ball so far as the game itself is concerned. . . . I know it is a better way for the average American to pass Sunday afternoon than many others resorted to by the average American for entertainment on that day. . . . I know the need of the money that is received for Sunday games by the management, especially of minor league clubs, whose gate receipts on weekdays are inadequate to meet expenses. All this I know, and yet I also know that it is of paramount importance that the laws of every city and state and country be respected and upheld; that the youth of every community should be educated to honor and obey the laws. And so whenever this problem presents itself for my decision, I first ask the question, "Is Sunday ball playing legal?" If it is, I say "Play Ball."[6]

But there was more to it than the law. In 1886, he still deemed that "strong sentiment among the better class against Sunday ball-playing" meant the team should not think of playing on the Sabbath.[7] Spalding was afraid that middle-class fans, who made up the bulk of weekday attendance, would disapprove of Sunday games and boycott the club's contests.[8] A few years later, when the law finally permitted it and it seemed safe business-wise, Spalding jumped at the opportunity of playing Sunday games in Chicago. The team in the early 1890s had moved to South Side Grounds, also known as Brotherhood Park, at 35th and Wentworth, site of the future Comiskey

Park. Spalding had moved the team because the railroad provided easier and faster transportation to the park and was near the grounds for the upcoming World's Fair.[9] In a fortuitous move that would help seal the team's financial success, the league had lifted its ban on Sunday games outright in 1892.[10] As luck would have it, however, the team's lease at South Side Grounds prevented Spalding from providing Sunday entertainment.[11] In 1893, after construction of a new elevated line to the West Side was announced, Spalding staged the first White Stockings Sunday game at the new West Side Grounds at what is now Polk and Wolcott, where crowds flocked to the Sabbath games. He kept the rest of the schedule on the South Side.[12]

That Sunday ball was a commercial success should have been expected. Attendance figures throughout the 1880s point to the earning potential of holiday sporting contests. Between 1882 and 1889, the Fourth of July home game was the highest draw of the season. The only exception was 1886, when there was no game scheduled because the fourth fell on a Sunday. Moreover Saturday, which most white-collar workers had off, was the day on which the greatest proportion of games were scheduled; they also were the games where attendance tended to be the highest.[13] Thus, the prospect of Sunday games was a tantalizing one for owners. James Hart, who in 1892 became the club's president—Spalding retaining a controlling interest—saw the move to Sunday games as a way to thwart possible competition by less scrupulous club owners. And, Hart added, if the Columbian Exposition could be opened for business on Sunday, so could the team.[14]

The team played Sundays without incident until 1895, when the Reverend W. W. Clark staged a showdown with the club over the issue. In 1893, Clark and his interdenominational International Sunday Observance League had protested the planned opening of the World's Fair on a Sunday.[15] The exposition officially kicked off on a Monday—May 1—but was open on Sundays during twenty-two of the fair's twenty-six weeks. Congress had included a non-Sunday clause in its appropriation, but after it reneged on a grant, the exposition's organizers considered themselves free to ignore the clause. Yet, the fair lost money on Sundays, possibly because many of the facilities did in fact close on those days, reducing the value of the entrance ticket.[16] The following year, the Observants turned their attention to baseball, but their pleas to shut down the games because they constituted a public nuisance fell on deaf ears at city hall and the courts.[17] On June

23, 1895, Clark tried again, this time after having secured the help of a sympathetic judge. The incident was a farce:

> Just before the game opened Umpire Galvin stood in front of the grand stand and taking off his hat and making his most polite bow announced:
> "The game will be delayed for five minutes after the third inning."
> Then he smiled sweetly and the crowd on the bleachers yelled.
> When the [side] had been retired for the third time, Capt. Anson called them to him and all trotted off to the club-house to be arrested and released on bail. The crowd waited patiently, and in less than five minutes play was resumed. There were fully 10,000 people on the ground and many of them were in the outfield. When the Colts went to be arrested several hundred of the spectators followed and made divers [sic] threats against the constables who had made the warrants, but President "Jim" Hart managed to quiet the Chicago sympathizers and the arrests went on.
> The whole thing had been carefully arranged. The warrants had been secured from Justice Cleveland of Norwood Park, and, besides the Colts, called for the appearance of Oliver Tabeau of the Clevelands. But as the latter did not play yesterday the papers were not served. Early in the day, the Rev. G.W. Clark took his stand upon the roof of a house overlooking the ball park. After he had seen some good ball playing he crawled down from his perch and the warrants were served. The complaints had been sworned out before Justice Cleveland of Norwood Park. He was on hand with a force of constables and was given a reserved seat in the club-house. President Hart had some other justices of the peace on hand to accept bail bonds in case Justice Cleveland should refuse, but he was willing and as fast as the players could sign they were released. The bonds were for $100 each.[18]

Two weeks later, in Norwood Park, Anson and his players appeared at a hearing, where E. F. Cornell, of 454 Wood Street, testified that

> he and his family were much disturbed by the noise of the ball game; so much so that he had gone upon the roof of his house and watched the game. Mr. Clark, who had been visiting at the house, had also been disturbed, and had joined him on the roof. He admitted that the players did not make the noise, and that to all appearances they were quiet and

orderly. The noise, he said, was made by the spectators, who clapped their hands and cheered the various plays.[19]

The team's attorney argued that if clapping or cheering constituted a nuisance, then all Sunday meetings should be forbidden.[20] On July 20, the Colts were found guilty of "noise, rout and amusement" on the Sabbath and were fined $3 each. The judge hinted that his decision would probably not stand in upper court, and the Colts declared they would continue to play on Sunday.[21] The next day, a Sunday, only 7,500 fans watched the Chicagos lose to the Brooklyns, a number a reporter attributed to the affair.[22] By early August, Sunday crowds were back to the usual ten thousand.[23] The club appealed the decision and in the fall it was thrown out.[24]

The legal battle did not occur in a vacuum. The same questions were being debated at City Hall by pietists and liberal aldermen. In 1894, the city council passed an ordinance to prohibit the opening of stores on Sunday. The long list of items not to be sold on that day included everything from hats to meat to furniture. But entertainment and baseball were not mentioned. The ordinance did state that "no person, firm, company or corporation [. . .] shall keep open for business within the city of Chicago [. . .] on the first day of the week, commonly called Sunday."

Holding that "the personal liberty of the private citizen is too sacred," Mayor John Hopkins vetoed the "paternalistic legislation." The right to do whatever one pleased on Sunday was legitimate, he wrote, "irrespective of the divine law, which enjoins us to remember the Sabbath and keep it holy." Hopkins refused to go beyond Illinois law, which held that worldly labor and employment were only prohibited "in case they disturb the peace and good order of society." It was on that point of law that Clark had tried to bring down Sunday baseball. The aldermen failed to override the veto. They later reintroduced an identical bill, which was reported to committee in January 1895 and shelved in April 1896.[25] Sunday now was a day for baseball.

"IT WAS STRAIGHT WHISKEY"

THE SETTLEMENT OF THE SUNDAY QUESTION was the culmination of years of a tense relationship between the club and the middle class it purported to emulate and entertain. When West Side Park opened in 1885, its affluent neighbors opposed it as a threat to the neighborhood's well-being.[1] The makeup of the neighborhood did change progressively over the next few years to include more immigrants.[2] Between 1890 and 1900, the eleventh ward's population increased from 35,000 to 37,500. By 1910, the figure would jump to 57,664. What had been in 1890 a community dominated by native whites with some immigrants at its north end was, twenty years later, almost half populated by newcomers, mostly from Austria, Russia, and Germany. The number of persons per dwelling had soared from 8.26 in 1890 to 12.8 by 1910. Similar trends took place in the nearby eighteenth and nineteenth wards.[3]

While fears about unsavory crowds and rampant gambling may have been for the most part unfounded, the game did retain an immoral dimension in the eyes of many. Prompted by letters from moral-minded "prominent citizens and patrons of the game"—as well as from vindictive personal enemies of his players and criticism in the press—Spalding had been forced early in the 1880s to address accusations of drunkenness and debauchery on the part of his White Stockings.

The team was winning games, so the players saw no justification for management's concern and asked, "What's the matter with our game?" Kelly

WHEN WHISKEY THREATENED

The stranglehold of liquor, as illustrated in Spalding's book on the history of baseball. (Author's collection)

even asked Spalding, "What are you running here? A Sunday School or a Base Ball Club?" To which Spalding recollected answering, "while we're not exactly in the Sunday School business, we would still like to have the boys reasonably clean in their habits."

Spalding hired Billy Pinkerton, a private detective, to keep an eye on his players' off-the-field activities. The ensuing report exonerated Cap Anson and several others. But emerging star Mike Kelly and six others had hobbies "too awful for patient consideration." Roaming Clark Street and the tenderloin district, the players spent their time in saloons and speakeasies. Mindful that if full National League sanctions were applied the team would be disseminated and out of contention, Spalding and Anson decided to take a more lenient approach. After they confronted the players about the report, all were silent, except for Kelly: "I have to offer only one amendment. In the place where the detective reports me as taking a lemonade at 3 A.M. he's off. It was straight whiskey; I never drank a lemonade at that hour in my life." Asked what they thought their penalty ought to be, the guilty players decided to pay the detective's fee. There's no evidence the players changed their ways immediately. When they next encountered one of Pinkerton's men, they confronted him and kicked him.[4]

By the time the White Stockings moved to the grounds at Harrison and Throop in 1885, Spalding had put in place a curfew for his players. In 1887, Spalding required a temperance pledge and players received bonuses if they stayed away from liquor altogether. This was done with the goal of "keeping up the reputation of the club," Spalding said. "We shall no longer endure the criticism of respectable people because of drunkenness in the Chicago nine. . . . We don't intend to again insult ladies and gentlemen of this city or any other by allowing men who are full of beer and whiskey to go upon the diamond in the uniform of the Chicago club."[5]

Whether it was in spite of the players' extracurricular antics or thanks to Spalding's rigorous enforcement, the neighborhood surrounding the ballpark did not become a cesspool of sin. In fact, property values rose.[6] The high rent paid by the club for the park's site—$7,500, more than five times the amount paid later at 35th and Wentworth—vouches for this.[7] The Reverend Thomas E. Green, pastor of the Eighth Presbyterian Church at 770 W. Lake (1959 W. Lake under the current street numbering system), located a few blocks north of the park, defended the presence of the team, which he asserted did not threaten the moral fiber of the community:

> Here we have had a ball game, distracting popular attention, filling the public prints—everybody talking and thinking of baseball. What a strange thing this life is. How easily influenced, how strangely excited, how quickly forgetting and hurrying along in the marvelous flight of time. . . . Ghostlike

solemnity has always posed as piety. . . . In spite of all this I choose to say there is a morality and a religion in amusement pure and simple. . . . I had sooner be childish in frivolity than torture myself trying to keep my neck stiff. . . . There is a great deal of sin in our constant neglect of our bodies. . . . As an amusement, [baseball] is in every way superior to nine-tenths of what we call amusements. People use it for gambling but men who want to gamble, if everything else failed, would bet on the weather. . . . It is not quite so dignified as some of the learned professions, but I had far rather be a good base ball player, and win the pennant for my club, than be a poor, dishonest merchant, constantly failing and swindling my creditors, or a briefless lawyer, hunting up divorce scandals for a livelihood. . . . I believe in sport, physical sport, in due measure and in rightful place, as a development of the body, a creator of health, a purifier of morals, a benefit to human life.[8]

God, as it happened, could be found at the ballpark. Literally. Utility outfielder Billy Sunday, a wickedly fast runner whom Anson had discovered in their common hometown of Marshalltown, Iowa, in 1883, was fairly weak at the bat, and his fielding was mediocre. But his fame would come a few years later as he left baseball to become one of the nation's most recognized preachers. Sunday recollected finding religion while playing for the White Stockings at West Side Park in a game against Detroit:

Two men were out and Detroit, with Charley Bennett at bat, had one man on second and another on third. He had two strikes on him and three balls called, when he fell on a ball with terrific force. It started for the clubhouse [deep in the outfield]. Benches had been placed in the field for spectators and as I saw the ball sailing through my section of the air I realized that it was going over the crowd, and I called, "Get out of the way." The crowd opened and as I ran I leaped those benches I said one of the swiftest prayers that was ever offered. It was: "Lord, if you ever helped a mortal man, help me get the ball." I went over the benches as though wings were carrying me up. I threw out my hand while in the air and the ball struck and stuck. The game was ours. Though the deduction is hardly orthodox, I am sure the Lord helped me catch that ball, and it was my first great lesson in prayer.[9]

Billy Sunday owed his major league career to his hailing from the same Iowa town as Cap Anson. Save for a banner year in 1887 when he batted .359, he never rose above .261 at the plate. His White Stockings fielding average over five seasons was .772. But it was in the Chicago outfield that he reportedly found God, becoming a famous preacher after four more underwhelming seasons with Pittsburgh and Philadelphia. (Author's collection)

Before too long, Sunday was doing much better with the collections plate than he had at home plate, making $7,000 a month as a preacher, which was more than ten times what he could have hoped to earn playing baseball.[10] Baseball imagery was peppered throughout his sermons, including this exhortation: "Oh Lord, give us some coachers out at this tabernacle so that people can be brought home to you. Some of them are dying on second and third base, Lord, and we don't want that." Righteous souls, Sunday once said, would be able to just "slide into heaven."[11]

Meanwhile, Spalding—for all his long-standing moralizing and grandstanding about the higher nature of baseball and, by extension, Spalding himself—was a moral fraud. The champion of Victorian values engaged in a years-long affair with a woman named Elizabeth Churchill and had a son with her. He eventually married Ms. Churchill after his wife died.[12]

"MIGHTY CASEY HAS STRUCK OUT"

SPALDING WAS EVEN MORE FORWARD than he had been the previous year in blaming the players for losing the 1886 title to St. Louis. He accused them of having drunk too much before games and denied them their bonuses for the year. Moreover, Spalding thought the team's fans were ready for "new blood" to replace "the same faces year after year."[1] He engineered what Anson called "a general shaking up along the line."[2]

Spalding had not forgiven Kelly for his arrogant attitude during the Pinkerton affair, convinced that "Kelly's habits were not conducive to the best interest of the club or his team-mates. . . . Particularly was his influence objectionable upon the younger members of the nine."[3] Kelly's habits would eventually prove harmful to Kelly himself, who would die three days shy of thirty-seven, after his drinking intensified to the point his last playing days in Boston were marred by inebriated play that saw him even fall down drunk a few times. Pneumonia would do him in, but the years of boozing likely made the King more vulnerable to it.[4]

For now, Kelly, however, was living up to his "King" nickname and played a major part in the team's recent successes. In his seven years with the White Stockings beginning in 1880, he had hit .316 over 681 games.[5] In 1886, he blasted 175 hits and scored 155 runs in just 118 games for a .388 batting average, his best to date. His wiliness made him a fan favorite. In a contest at Boston, he won the game for Chicago in the twelfth inning, the Red Stockings having loaded the bases with two outs: "It was growing very dark. In this crucial spot, the Boston batter hit a long, hard drive in Kelly's direction. Mike could not see the ball at all, but realized that the umpire was probably in the same fix. He ran back, posed alertly, waited a moment, leaped into the air with a wild whoop, and pantomimed a catch. He then ran for the clubhouse as if the game was over, and the umpire, completely fooled, yelled, 'Out.'"[6]

In a game against Detroit, Kelly snatched a Chicago run out of a certain inning-ending play at home plate. With the score tied at two, Kelly feigned injury after sliding into third base and asked teammate Ed Williamson, who was at second base, for help getting up. When the latter approached, Kelly whispered "Say, Ed, as soon as Weidman [the pitcher] raises his arm, I'm going to make a break for home, and you sneak along behind me. They'll play me, sure, and forget about you; but when I'm close I'll straddle me legs, and you slide under."[7] Kelly took off for home at the pitch and surprised the catcher by stopping a few feet short of the plate. Meanwhile, Williamson cut third base by fifteen feet and scored, avoiding the tag by sliding through Kelly's legs.[8]

Anson credited Kelly with inventing the "hit and run" and being the first to use the fade-away or hook slide, which became known as the "Chicago" slide. Years later, in 1899, Kelly would be spoofed in "Slide, Kelly, Slide," the most successful baseball song until "Take Me Out to the Ball Game" a decade later.[9]

In a 1982 article for the *Smithsonian,* James Cox documented the full breadth of Kelly's innovations:

- First outfielder to back up his infielders.
- First right fielder to take a line drive on the bounce and throw out the batter at first base—a rather exciting play still.
- First catcher to set up battery signals with his pitcher, and to signal the fielders what the pitcher would throw next.
- Inventor of the hit-and-run play (this was erroneously credited to the old Baltimore Orioles, who made good use of it but did not create it).
- Innovator of the practice of having pitchers and catchers back up infielders to protect against overthrows to the various bases.
- First catcher to intentionally drop the new "birdcage" mask on the plate, or toss it in the path of an incoming runner to trip him or scare him or at least slow him up—not a glowing accomplishment but a typical Kelly ploy that won a few games.[10]

Kelly was not only one of the most prominent Irish players of his time but has since been dubbed by some as Babe Ruth before Babe Ruth. He is said to have been the inspiration for one of the most famous pieces of baseball poetry, Ernest Lawrence Thayer's 1888 "Casey at the Bat." Whether or not he inspired it, Kelly appropriated it. He took to reciting it in vaudeville shows, and the poem routinely got printed as "Kelly at the Bat."[11]

CASEY (KELLY) AT THE BAT

The outlook wasn't brilliant for the Mudville nine that day;
The score stood four to two, but with but one inning more to play;
And so, when Cooney died at first, and Burrows did the same;
A sickly silence fell upon the patrons of the game.

A struggling few got up to go in deep despair, the rest
Clung to the hope which springs eternal in the human breast;
They thought, if only Casey could but get a whack, at that,
They'd put up even money now—with Casey at the bat.

But Flynn preceded Casey, as did also Jimmy Blake,
And the former was a pudding and the latter a cake;
So upon that stricken multitude grim melancholy sat,
For there seemed but little chance of Casey's getting to the bat.

But Flynn let drive a single, to the wonderment of all,
And Blake, the much despised, tore the cover off the ball;
And when the dust had lifted, and they saw what had occurred,
There was Jimmy safe on second, and Flynn a-hugging third.

Then from the gladdened multitude went up a joyous yell,
It bounded from the mountain-top, and rattled in the dell;
It struck upon the hillside, and recoiled upon the flat;
For Casey, mighty Casey, was advancing to the bat.

There was ease in Casey's manner as he stepped into his place;
There was pride in Casey's bearing and a smile on Casey's face;
And when, responding to the cheers, he lightly doffed his hat,
No stranger in the crowd could doubt 'twas Casey at the bat.

Ten thousand eyes were on him as he rubbed his hands with dirt,
Five thousand tongues applauded when he wiped them on his shirt;
Then while the writhing pitcher ground the ball into his hip,
Defiance gleamed in Casey's eye, a sneer curled Casey's lip.

Shown in a late 1880s cartoon, Mike "King" Kelly was one of base-ball's first "crossover" superstars, immortalized in song and poem. His .316 average as a Cub did not earn him much respect from Spalding, who sent him packing to Boston in 1887. He had challenged Spalding's attempts to clean up the personal lives of his players, but the main reason he was sold away was because Spalding had negotiated a record price for him. (Author's collection)

And now the leather covered sphere came hurtling through the air,
And Casey stood a-watching it, a haughty grandeur there;
Close by the sturdy batsmen the ball unheeded sped,
"That ain't my style," said Casey; "Strike One" the umpire said.

From the benches, black with people, there went a muffed roar,
Like the beating of the storm-waves on a stern and distant shore;
"Kill him: Kill the umpire!" shouted some one in the stand,
And it's likely they'd have killed him, had not Casey raised his hand.

With a smile of Christian charity great Casey's visage shone;
He stilled the rising tumult; he bade the game go on;
He signaled to the pitcher, and once more the spheroid flew,
But Casey still ignored it, and the umpire said "Strike Two."

"Fraud!" cried the maddened thousands, and the echo answered "fraud!"
But a scornful look from Casey, and the audience was awed;
They saw his face grow stern and cold, they saw his muscles strain.
And they knew that Casey wouldn't let the ball go by again.

The sneer is gone from Casey's lips, his teeth are clenched in hate,
He pounds with cruel violence his bat upon the plate;
And now the pitcher holds the ball, and he lets it go,
And now the air is shattered by the force of Casey's blow.

Oh! somewhere in this favored land the sun is shining bright,
The band is playing somewhere, and somewhere hearts are light;
And somewhere men are laughing, and somewhere children shout;
But there is no joy in Mudville—mighty Casey has struck out.[12]

There certainly was no joy in Chicago when it was announced that Spalding had in fact sold Kelly to Boston. Spalding exceeded Kelly's expectations by securing a $5,000-a-year salary for him, $2,000 more than what Chicago had paid. But the real coup was that Spalding had really sold Kelly to the Red Stockings for $10,000—the most money ever for a player[13]—pocketing $5,000 in the deal. For Boston to fall for the trick, which would benefit both men, Kelly had to "play the 'poor Base Ball slave,'" which he did to the limit.[14] The newspapers accused Spalding of compromising the team's chances at a third pennant, arguing that if the White Stockings were to have cheap players, the price of admission should be reduced.[15]

But Spalding knew better; money and winning did not necessarily go hand in hand. The team had lost Kelly, Gore, and McCormick—who were also part of Spalding's wholesale liquidation.[16] But there were enough veterans on the team to be competitive, and Chicago finished third in 1887, six-and-a-half games behind Detroit, which went on to avenge the National League by beating the Browns 10-5 in the "Champions of the World" series.[17] Anson hit an astounding .421, thanks to a one-year experiment under which a walk was counted as a base hit. Adjusted, his batting average still led the team with .347. No other player hit more than .300. Clarkson, ever the workhorse, posted a 38-21 record on the mound. Upon Kelly's first road trip to Chicago with Boston, a large crowd awaited him at his hotel, and a local reporter marveled that "President Cleveland, or even the queen herself, could hardly have had a more flattering ovation."[18] Boston, with its new star Kelly, finished near the bottom of the standings, prompting Anson to say that "'One swallow does not make a summer,' however, nor one ball player a whole team."[19] Kelly, though, had not slowed down, batting .391 and slamming 211 hits in '87. The attacks on Spalding in the press were vociferous, the sportswriters seeing a clear link between Kelly's departure and the team's subpar season.

> While these daily "roasts" were being served out to me I noticed that the attendance kept increasing. . . . I happened to meet [hostile baseball writer "Harmony"] White on the street one day, early in the summer, and asked him:
>
> "What's the matter with the *News*? You haven't been giving me the usual amount of space of late."
>
> He replied that he was absolutely *out of ammunition*. I offered to furnish him fresh ammunition if he would only keep up the onslaught. . . . I then explained to him that simply as a business proposition I could not afford to be neglected in his paper, for since he had let up in his attacks our attendance was dropping off.[20]

Spalding fed "ammunition" to the writer twice a week for the remainder of the season; his third-place team made more money than ever and shattered all attendance records. Two-hundred seventeen thousand fans came to West Side Park to see the Kelly-less Stockings, an average of 3,558 a game. In October, the club's stockholders received a dividend of 20 percent, thanks to $100,000 in profits the team had made in just a few years.[21]

As "less is more" proved profitable, Spalding sent Clarkson to join Kelly in Boston at the end of the season, pocketing an additional $10,000. He saved more money by refusing to renegotiate Pfeffer's contract, who demanded a raise or else he would leave. But Spalding was unmoved, "A player growling and grumbling, and saying he is dissatisfied, and will refuse to play with a club is simply bash. . . . He will play here or no where."[22] Pfeffer agreed to Spalding's terms.

Spalding's tough stance was informed by his deep belief that baseball players should be thankful for even the lowest salaries paid by teams. The editorial comment section of his 1894 guide mentioned that players had complained about "cut-rate" salaries and threatened to go into business if they were not given higher salaries. Arguing that star players made $75 to $100 per week, Spalding asked: "What star player was there in the ranks who was competent to earn $50 a week in any ordinary business vocation? In fact, the majority of the players could not have earned even $25 a week in any business vocation to save their lives. Look at the fools who, by sacrificing themselves at the altar of Bacchus, have forfeited their chance to earn salaries as baseball players, and who are glad to even earn a dollar a day for ten hours of hard labor." Players, of course, disagreed. In fact, John Ward, the president of the Brotherhood of Professional Base Ball Players when it began in 1885, argued the Players League (born from the Brotherhood) had proved otherwise: "The conduct of the men has thoroughly refuted the National League's declaration that the baseball player was not able to do business for himself."[23]

Kelly became an owner-manager of the new league's Boston team. Spalding was dispatched to entice Kelly back to the National League with $25,000, with the assumption that a defection by the star would do the Players League in. Kelly, broke, still passed, telling Spalding "I can't go back on the boys." Spalding, spurned but uncharacteristically kind, handed him $500.[24]

Four years later, on November 9, 1894, the *Boston Daily Globe* reported, "last night 'King Kelly' heard the decision of the Great Umpire from which there is no appeal." Anson eulogized him: "Kelly invariably played ball for the good of his team, and in this way injured his individual batting, fielding and catching record." But Cap also concluded that Kelly had had "one enemy . . . himself."[25]

BASEBALL MISSIONARIES

WITH CLARKSON GONE, the pitching load was spread around in 1888. Gus Krock appeared in thirty-eight games, winning twenty-four. The White Stockings used eleven pitchers altogether. Again, Anson led the team at the plate with .344. Jimmy Ryan had 182 hits, which translated into a .332 batting average. He hit for the cycle on July 28. The team was head and shoulders above most of the league but could not overcome New York, which finished nine games ahead with a phenomenal team ERA of 1.96. In keeping with the Spalding touch, the team did again very well at the gate, with 229,863 fans, or 3,380 per game.[1]

In spite of the rankings, the White Stockings, not the New York Giants, would be the league's uncontested stars in October. Spalding had arranged for his team and an assortment of "All-Americans" to embark on a world tour—really a trip to Australia and back—to promote the game. The journey had several goals, some more openly stated than others. The first was to introduce the sport to the rest of the world, which meant exposing other peoples to the righteousness and wholesomeness of the game—and America. Therefore, Spalding handpicked the "All Americans" to ensure that no "undesirable players in the fraternity" were included. The tour would also, Spalding hoped, help the game make further inroads in the United States; he arranged for a contingent of newspapermen from New York and Chicago to travel with the teams.[2] Although he was quieter about it, Spalding thought the endeavor might improve his business prospects as well, in Chicago and elsewhere. If all went well, he would be "extending [his sporting goods] business to that quarter of the globe."[3]

Spalding and a few investors, Anson among them, put together $50,000 for the trip, but the planning was left to Spalding and Leigh S. Lynch, a New York businessman.[4] During the White Stockings' last eastern trip of the season, Chicago congressman Frank Lawler arranged for a meeting between Anson and his players and President Grover Cleveland, who wished them luck on their upcoming journey.[5] After a farewell game in front of three thousand at the West Side Grounds on October 20, 1888, the teams left for San Francisco.[6] On the way, they played exhibition games in parts of the country where major league baseball had yet to tread: St. Paul in front of two thousand, Cedar Rapids in front of forty-five hundred, then Des Moines, Omaha, Denver, Sacramento, and Salt Lake City. Attendance was modest, but Spalding recalled that everywhere the "Base Ball Missionaries received standing ovations."[7]

On November 18, they sailed from San Francisco for a pilgrimage of sorts in Hawaii, where Alexander Cartwright, of Knickerbockers fame, had taken residence. Unable to play a game because of local Sunday laws, they headed for Auckland, New Zealand, where they arrived on December 10. Then it was on to Sydney and Melbourne, where ten thousand watched the Americans peddle their sport.[8]

The *Melbourne Argus* marveled at the Americans, "stalwarts every man, lumps of muscle showing beneath their tight fitting jersey garments. . . . [I]f base ball had anything to do with building up such physique we ought to encourage it." After playing the American all-stars, the Chicagos played local cricketers. Melbourne's *Sportsman* newspaper relayed that "A man may be able to guard a wicket with a degree of skill that would win him wide fame in cricket circles, but when it comes to standing beside the home plate of a base ball diamond, and mastering the terrific delivery of an American professional pitcher, the average cricketer is compelled to acknowledge the wide difference existing between the two positions."[9]

Finding that the distance from Australia around the World to New York was about the same as via San Francisco, Spalding proposed a return trip through Africa and Europe. So the missionaries rang in the New Year playing in front of "startled" natives in Ceylon. The forty-five hundred curious British subjects there would be one of the best turnouts of the rest

Spalding's baseball missionaries played a game in the shadow of the Sphinx and great pyramids, with a very sparse crowd of local spectators and their dromedaries. The drawing of the same event in Spalding's autobiography showed a larger crowd. (Author's collection)

of the tour, for sure more than the few bedouins who looked on as the teams posed for a picture on the Sphinx in Egypt and played a game at the foot of the pyramids.

In February, Anson and the All-Americans "showed the Italians how to play the great American game" in Rome, Naples, and Florence before heading for France, where a game near the Eiffel Tower delighted the American colony. The French, however, "did not seem to catch on to any appreciable extent."[10]

Only in England did Spalding receive the sort of treatment—fit for baseball royalty—he had hoped to get in the other countries. Several Dukes and Earls were on hand for a reception at the Surrey County Cricket Club. Spalding's careful selection of the All-Americans a few months earlier came in handy as the English hosts were "astonished" to see baseball players "not only attired in full evening dress, but with a degree of social familiarity with social requirements that was quite foreign to professional cricketers."[11] But the local sportsmen had the last laugh when the Prince of Wales and the king attended a wet and foggy exhibition game at which Spalding broke court etiquette—"I must plead that I was not at court, but at an American ball game"—by sitting next to the king and touching his royal person. It was at the end of that game that the prince made his famous remark, "I consider Base Ball an excellent game; but Cricket a better one."[12]

All told, sixty thousand saw the baseball exhibitions throughout the British Isles, but the American ballplayers would have to wait until their return to New York in April to receive the kind of adulation to which they had been accustomed. At a banquet there, a guest declared, "Washington never saw a base-ball game; Madison wrote the Constitution without seeing one . . . I feel as I stand here that all the men that have ever lived and achieved success in this world have died in vain."[13]

The teams made their way back to Chicago by way of Baltimore, Washington—where Benjamin Harrison was much less enthused about baseball as his predecessor, giving Anson and his men a very chilly reception—Pittsburgh, and Cleveland. At Chicago's Union Station, the crowd was a "howling, yelling mob, and as we entered our carriages and the procession moved up Wabash Ave. and across Harmon Court to Michigan Ave., amid the bursting of rockets, the glare of calcium lights and Roman candles, we felt that we were indeed at home again."[14] More than 150,000 lined the streets to greet the returning baseball evangelists. Not surprisingly, Spalding pronounced Chicago "the sweetest, dearest place on this globe."[15]

THE LEAN YEARS

WHEN THEY ONCE AGAIN TOOK THE FIELD against their National League rivals for the 1889 season, the White Stockings were never in the running for the pennant. Shortstop Ned Williamson could not come back to form after knee problems stemming from the world tour. Gus Krock, who had led the pitching staff the previous year, developed arm trouble. Although Anson picked up where he left off with a .342 batting average, the team finished third behind New York and Boston. Though that finish was honorable in a field of eight teams, Chicago was nineteen games out of first and eighteen out of second. For the first time in more than ten years, the Whites were barely a .500 club.[1] Chicago fans were beginning to grow frustrated with the team, which only drew 149,175, a drop of more than one thousand per game from the previous year.[2]

For the next two years, the team contended for the pennant in a league from which talent had been severely drained by the new Players' League.[3] Fred Pfeffer was among those who, fed up with the arbitrary salary caps and poor treatment at the hands of unscrupulous owners, had taken part a mass exodus to the rival league in 1890 in what would come to be known as the Brotherhood War.

Anson was left with a bunch of green players, who quickly earned the moniker of Colts. In March, with the season still weeks away, the team went on a trip through the South, playing exhibition games in Chattanooga, At-

By June 3, 1887, the *Chicago Daily News* already knew the White Stockings were headed into oblivion. The championship drought would last nineteen seasons. (Author's collection)

lanta, Augusta, and Mobile.[4] Anson and Spalding were just catching up to the growing trend of spring training, which had gone on for several years.[5]

The team managed second-place finishes in '90 and '91. But the White Stockings faced their toughest competition off the field. For the first time, the team had competition in Chicago in the persons of the Pirates, who played many games at Brotherhood Park.[6] In his memoirs Spalding recalled "no one cared for the score of yesterday's game; nobody looked for the championship record of 1890. All eyes were centered on the question of attendance."[7] At a time of "meager" attendance for the Colts and "more popularly attended" Pirates contests, Spalding sent spies to his rivals' games to count heads. The revelation by Spalding that Brotherhood attendance was inflated—never mind that it was still much higher than the National

League's—served as a diversion to hide his own team's woes. After averaging more than two thousand per game the preceding year, the team sometimes drew fewer than fifty fans. After months of playing two games—"Base ball and bluff"—Spalding and the Brotherhood ended the feud, the Brotherhood teams merging with the NL squads.[8]

Spalding had achieved a lot more than the death of a rival league. The capitulation of the Players' League also meant that the salary controls instigated by Spalding—which had led to the creation of the rebel league in the first place—would continue to be enforced. It would take almost twenty years for the highest cost paid for a player to get back to the level of $10,000 paid by Boston for Kelly in 1889. After that, however, all bets would be off. In 1911, Marty O'Toole was signed by Pittsburgh for $22,500 and in 1914 Johnnie Evers went to Boston for $25,000.

Eager to capitalize on the South Side's appeal as home of the upcoming 1893 World's Fair, Spalding scheduled half his team's games at Brotherhood Park in 1891—where he rented from the Players' League, at one-fifth the cost of the Congress site. Attendance was markedly better on the South Side, and the "west side cranks lost bid to keep some games." By 1892, the Congress Street site was totally abandoned, ending the first chapter in the history of major league baseball on Chicago's West Side.[9]

The lingering American Association was dead, owing in part to the Brotherhood's impact on its attendance. Four association teams joined the National League. In 1892 the Colts, with a dismal team batting average of .236, finished seventh in the field of twelve. Anson batted under .300 for the second straight season after thirteen years of hitting above that mark. Bill Hutchison, a right-handed Colt who made a name for himself by going 42-25 in 1890 and 43-19 in 1891, showed signs of overwork. Anson relied on him very heavily, calling on him to pitch in more than 1,110 innings in those two years. In '92, Hutchison fell to 37-34, logging in his third year of five-hundred-plus innings.

BACK TO THE WEST SIDE

WITH FALTERING HITTERS AND TIRING PITCHERS, the team finished twenty-nine games behind Boston in 1883. Owing to the success of his Sunday baseball experiment at West Side Grounds that year, Spalding moved all of the team's games to Polk and Wood streets for the 1894 season. The Metropolitan west side elevated, on the path of the future I-294, would soon facilitate the trip to the ballpark when it opened in 1895, and even more so when the line hooked up with the Loop L in 1897.[1]

The new $30,000 stadium had a majesty missing from the team's previous homes. For the first time, the playing field was completely enclosed by stands. Home plate was near the corner of Polk and Lincoln, now Wolcott Avenue. The right field wall, 340 feet from home, came up against a row of homes and shops fronting Taylor. Left field, on the Wood Street side, was also 340 feet deep. Five hundred sixty feet into centerfield stood the scoreboard, above the brick clubhouse.[2]

But the rest of the stadium was made of wood. On August 5, 1894, in the seventh inning, the grandstand behind home plate caught fire, generating a stampede that injured hundreds. Players used their bats to open a path for the panicking crowd through barbed wire put up for crowd containment.[3]

Just as around Wrigley Field later, the roofs of residences across the street made for good viewing. On July 17, 1908, a fourteen-year-old boy watching from what were then called "housetop grandstands" on Wood Street would jump for joy over a Joe Tinker home run and fall fifty feet, fracturing his skull.

CHAPTER 15

West Side Grounds as seen in a 1909 postcard. (Courtesy Brian Bernardoni)

The tragedy came as the City of Chicago and building owners across from the ballpark were in court over safety issues. The boy died at the nearby county hospital, and the judge in the ongoing case enjoined building owners at 440 and 451 Wood Street and 783 W. Taylor Street to stop using the grandstands (under today's numbering system, those buildings were in the 1800–1900 block of West Taylor and the 800–900 block of South Wood). The *Chicago Tribune* reported that the housetop grandstands had been a "bone of contention between building owners and city officials for years."[4] The team tried to get the rooftop bleachers, also called housetop grandstands, across the street removed to cut down on the competition, which charged five to ten cents a seat. In the end, the City only regulated them, allowing them on fireproof buildings with an adequate means of escape, which forced modification of the Cubs own roof stand but allowed several rooftops across the street to remain. The Cubs erected a wall along the right field bleachers that eventually reached eighty feet and blocked the view for some, but not all, of its neighboring competitors.[5]

Although the team played at its worst through the '90s, the spectators kept flooding through the gates, planting the seed for later tradition of being lovable and profitable losers. On May 3, 1896, the overflow crowd was so large that it interfered with the game. On April 30, 1899, reportedly the largest crowd in baseball history, 27,489, gathered at West Side Grounds.[6] Accordingly, gate receipts were high, and the team generated 20 to 25 percent in profits between 1895 and 1901.[7] Yet for nine long years, the Colts would never come close to contention. Their highest finish came in 1895, when they were fourth, fifteen games out of first.

In 1896, a plan by Spalding to play night games fell through, but he used the lights he had already erected to provide amusement park rides in the evening.[8] Spalding's business fortunes continued to rise with those of the team and the league. In 1892 his company had a capitalization of $4 million, up from the $800 start-up money his mother had lent him and his brother sixteen years earlier.[9]

By then, most of the "modern" rules of baseball were in place. In 1845, the Knickerbockers' rule book set the object of the game as being the first team to score twenty-one runs, regardless of the number of innings, which was finally set at nine in 1857. Pitching witnessed the largest number of rule changes. There were no called balls until the National Association of Base Ball Players introduced the concept in 1863, at the same time it denied pitchers the right to run or step to the right or left before delivering the ball. But, even then, much was left to the discretion of the umpires. Only after the pitcher failed to get the ball over the plate in a "reasonable number of the tries" did the umpire warn him and start counting balls. In 1867, things got even stranger with the decision to grant batters the right to request either a low pitch or a high pitch, a rule that would stand for twenty years. To make matters worse for pitchers, in 1872 it was decided that any called ball actually hit by the batter could not result in an out.

Once the umpire deigned beginning to count balls, the batter walked after the third called ball. In 1878, to restore some parity between hitter and hurler, the number of balls was fixed at nine, before being brought down to eight in 1880 and seven in 1881. After fluctuating between six and seven in the mid-80s, the number was set at five in 1887 and finally settled at four in 1889. The early 1840s rules required pitchers to do just that—pitch. That meant only underhand throws were accepted until 1883, when the curve ball, which pitchers sneaked by umpires for years, was legalized, albeit with the stipulation that the arm not be raised over the shoulder. The following year, all restrictions on the pitching motion were lifted. The mound, for many years located forty-five feet from home plate, was set at today's sixty-feet six inches in 1893 after being briefly located at fifty feet after 1881. The adoption of the foul ball as a strike unless the batter had two strikes against him would not be adopted until 1901.[10]

Among the large crowds at West Side Grounds during the losing 1890s was L. Frank Baum, who in 1897 would publish *Mother Goose in Prose* and in 1900 *The Wonderful Wizard of Oz*. Baum lived at 120 Flournoy Street (now 2149 W. Flournoy), a couple of blocks from West Side Grounds, and the roar of the crowd could be heard from the house. He was a frequent visitor to the ballpark.[11] Baum had moved to Chicago in May 1891, just in time to see the last good season of the great team of the 1880s.[12] In the five seasons between Baum's arrival in the city and the publication of "Two Pictures," his poem about fandom at West Side Grounds published three weeks into the 1896 season in the *Chicago News-Herald,* Anson and his men went 337-333. Still, Baum was obviously a fan, and in his 1911 book *Aunt Jane's Nieces and Uncle John,* written under the pen name of Edith Van Dyne, the male character's name is Anson Jones, or Uncle Anson, just like in the poem.[13]

"TWO PICTURES"

I.

With one tremendous, deaf'ning roar
Ten thousand throats proclaim
Chicago has the biggest score,
And Anson's won a game!

Ten thousand hats are toss'd in air,
Their owners all aflame
With rapture, for they're well aware
That "Uncle's" won a game.

Throughout the city flies the news
That tells the city's fame,
While pandemonium ensues—
For Anson's won a game!

All business worries are forgot,
E'en politics seem tame;
Who care for Cuba's woes a jot
Since Anson's won a game?

II.

But hark! what means this muttered growl,
This darksome look, this lowering scowl?
This "rooter's" ceased his joyous howl
And hangs his head in shame.

And o'er the city falls a gloom
Unequated save in gruesome tomb;
The reason is, we've met our doom
And Anson's lost a game!

FROM COLTS TO CUBS

IN SPITE OF A RESURGENCE IN 1894, when he hit .395, Anson clearly was slipping, at least in his own eyes. In 1897, after announcing it would be his last year as a player, he hit "only" .302, the third-lowest total of his twenty-two-year career. That was still good for fifth among position players, and he ranked third in RBIs. But that number, along with his run production, was down. He did set several historical marks that year: he became the game's first three-thousand-hit player and, at forty-six, the oldest man to hit above .300. Anson had learned to make fun of his own age, and to disarm his detractors in the process. Late in the 1891 season, he played an entire game with a false white mustache and wig. The team started the "Day" tradition with a Cap Anson Day on May 4, 1897. Anson hung it up as a .331 career hitter. The wise Cap walked 952 times to his 294 strikeouts in 2,276 games. As manager from 1879 on, he compiled a 1288-944 (.577) record.[1]

Although Anson recognized he had lost his edge as a player, he wanted to remain as skipper, a position he felt he had more than earned. Spalding and many fans surely felt otherwise, given the team's record in the '90s. In fact, Anson had lost his grip on the team. Players routinely went to the horse races instead of attending practice. Blinded by optimism and his love for the team, he repeatedly bet his team would win it all, using his team owner-ship as collateral. Team president Hart later pronounced Anson's shares so encumbered by gambling debts and loans as to be worthless. He admitted himself having "been too soft for a long time" on his players.[2]

Even Anson could not argue with the Colts' results. Even though he invoked some bad breaks, he glumly summed up the 1897 season in a Cleveland newspaper: "The Colts were not batting, fielding or running bases but otherwise they were all right." The *Chicago Tribune* welcomed the end of the season as "a relief." This was not a good thing for a player-manager coming to the end of a ten-year contract.[3]

His seemingly unavoidable departure from the club was a drawn-out, public drama that unfolded in the *Chicago Tribune* for months. In mid-September 1897, he told a reporter that he could print Anson would be back leading the Colts in 1898.[4] Rumors about him being pushed out had been circulated and amplified, and were not put to rest by a huge October 23 headline in the *Tribune* that proclaimed, "Anson Still a Colt—Wild rumor of his release proves unfounded." On November 10, the paper reported Anson and Hart had not been seen speaking to each other at the NL's annual meeting, and the next day it declared Anson was "likely to go" and be replaced by old "stonewall infield" member Tom Burns. On December 18, asked about his possible retirement, Anson said, "You'll have to ask Spalding," who said, "You'll have to ask Hart." On December 26, the *Tribune* announced Anson would resign on New Year's Day and Spalding, perhaps trying to soften the blow, announced short-lived plans for a "baseball college" in Chicago to train new players under the direction of Anson. New Year's Day came and went and on January 13 the paper promised that "definite news about the Colts is forthcoming." On the twenty-fourth, tired of waiting for team management and bowing to the obvious, the paper ran a retrospective of Burns's career to reintroduce the prospective manager to readers. Management could not seem to quite muster the nerve to make anything official but, the *Tribune* concluded, "If sentiment could win pennants Chicago would keep him forever and win, but he is to be sacrificed to reality."[5]

Never on very good terms with Spalding, Cap was even more hostile to James Hart, whom Spalding had made his puppet club president earlier in the decade. On February 1, 1898, Hart put out a statement saying the stockholders had voted not to renew Anson's contract, to which the deposed skipper answered somewhat pathetically that he had yet to make up his mind as to what *he* would do. Cap then made approaches about buying the team from Spalding and Hart, and the two demanded a price for their shares inflated by 50 percent. Anson, Spalding said, could have the club for $150,000. Though he tried, there was no way Anson could raise the money and, humiliated and bitter, he left the club to open a billiards hall just a few blocks from the ballpark after a disastrously short-lived stint as manager of the New York Giants. For the next three years, the team would be known as the Orphans.[6]

To this day, Anson is the Cubs' all-time leader in hits, runs, singles, doubles, and runs batted in. He still owns four of the top-ten all-time Cubs season batting averages, and his .331 team career average ranks third all-time. He ranks second to Ernie banks in all-time games and at-bats as a Cub. His five pennants as a manager (1880–1882, 1885–1886) remain a franchise record.

Anson's postbaseball career was adventurous and colorful and, if eventually a relative failure, it was never far from the limelight. After publishing his autobiography in 1900, he unsuccessfully tried his hand at several business ventures besides the billiards hall, and even was the president of a stillborn baseball league designed to challenge the National League's treatment of players. "The National League, which has been running baseball into the ground for the last eight years, will have opposition at one time or another," he said.[7] But the American League, founded in 1899, would be that counterweight, not Anson's own league.

He won the bowling national title after that, but it was baseball that still had his heart. Anson considered buying the Washington Senators in 1904 but the finances did not make sense, even for him. Instead, he was drafted to run for city clerk in 1905 on the Democratic ticket. His old prejudices were among his qualifications at a time when Democrats were accused of being soft on the race issue. The *Chicago Tribune* ran an editorial describing his stance as an opponent of "race suicide," the trend under which whites were having fewer children than blacks.[8]

Anson struck out as an elected official. When reformers ended the practice whereby the city clerk took a share of fees collected by his office as a bonus, he complained that it was unfair. There was some truth to it, considering other city offices got to keep the privilege; nonetheless, this was the first of several instances when he exercised poor judgment and misread public sentiment. He failed to crack down on his employees' rampant absenteeism (echoing his inability to reign in players in the 1890s) and was widely blamed for it by the city's Civil Service Commission, which according to press reports had to explain "the most elementary principles of government to Anson." In the midst of that scandal, he ran in the Democratic primary for sheriff. The *Chicago Tribune* editorialized that "cowardice is not a good qualification for another job." He received only twenty-two of one thousand votes at the nominating convention.[9]

Anson even created a mini constitutional crisis in 1907 by agreeing as city clerk to a request by mayor-elect Fred Busse to sign paperwork that resulted in the new mayor's term starting early. For nine days, thanks to Anson, Chicago had two mayors, Busse and lame duck Edward Dunne.[10]

With the government post gone, so was his $5,000 annual salary. His saving grace should have been that he had retained a significant stake in the National League Chicago franchise, with more than 10 percent of total shares. But new owner Jim Hart had not paid dividends in years. In December 1905, when Charles Murphy bought the team from Hart and Anson, he paid only $76.92 a share, well shy of the $150 price Spalding had offered to Anson a few years earlier, a clear sign Spalding had inflated the number to push Cap out.[11]

Once again, Anson turned to baseball for salvation. In 1907, he launched a semipro team called Anson's Colts and even built a small ballpark for it at 61st Street and St. Lawrence Avenue, using his house and business as collateral. With the team badly outdrawn by teams like the Logan Squares, Anson, at fifty-five years and 270 pounds, took to the field but even that "novelty" failed to right the course. Halfway through the season, creditors forced him to give up control of the home stadium of Anson's Colts, though Anson continued as manager and player.[12]

Desperate for funds, Anson even went back on his long-standing policy to refuse playing against black teams. In 1908, Anson's Colts would win the city title but get badly beaten in an exhibition match by a bunch of prospects and bench-warmers from the NL franchise. The team lost money again. This would cost him his house.[13] Amid his personal travails and in spite of his railings against his old team and the league, Anson was invited to throw out the first pitch in the 1908 season opener, which must have warmed his aging heart.[14] His glee is evident in pictures of the event.

Throughout his various postmanagerial ventures, Anson appeared occasionally on local vaudeville stages, though in this area too he could never rekindle past glory. In 1895, Charles Hoyt had written *A Runaway Colt*, designed to be a starring vehicle for Anson. After a successful run in Chicago in December, the play moved to Broadway for one month. In it, Anson tried to convince a recalcitrant family—dad was a preacher—to let their son become a professional baseball player. True to the times and to Anson's own prejudices, the play contained a racist remark about a White Stockings mascot, likely Clarence Duval. After several contretemps, Anson made everything all right by, what else, hitting a home run. For his first and last appearance on Broadway, Cap was declared in the *New York Dramatic Mirror* "quite as good as most people on stage with him," which was not saying much of the rest of the cast given that Anson was described as delivering his lines "with the directness of an artillery officer, no matter whether he is accepting an invitation to dinner or defending the good cause of professional baseball." Anson had his own assessment, captured on his red-lettered stationery: "A better actor than any ball player, a better ball player than any actor."[15]

Anson was inducted into the Hall of Fame in 1939, seventeen years after his death in 1922.[16]

The 1898 season, under new manager Tom Burns, of the old "stonewall infield" under Anson, offered a glimmer of hope with an 85-75 record, but the team soon settled back into mediocrity with a .507 showing in 1899, good for eighth out of twelve teams. The club's only true moment in the sun that season came before the first game, when Burns and his men replaced their spring training at West Baden, Indiana, with a trip to Hudson Springs in New Mexico for a boot camp that, the *Tribune* reported, consisted mostly of "bronco riding, mountain climbing, and long hunting trips" that made the players "hard as rocks."[17] True to form, Spalding was likely mixing sport and business in organizing the trip; the resort where the team stayed was owned by Chicagoan Andrew Graham, who reportedly had put much effort into growing it at the prodding of Spalding.[18]

The nadir in team history up to that point came in 1901, when it finished with a paltry .381 winning percentage. Newspaper reports on the team's efforts included such headlines as "suffer their usual defeat." By far the worst showing ever to that point, it would not be "bested" until 1962, when the team was under the ill-fated leadership of the so-called College of Coaches. The reason the team went from below average (.464 in 1900) to awful was a mass defection from Anson's Orphans to the new American League, earning the team the name Remnants in the papers. Three of the "traitors" went

Cap Anson's grave in Oakwoods Cemetery in Chicago. Given the family's finances, only the small marker was placed there at the funeral. Former players and friends raised funds for the larger monument, which states, "He Played the Game." (Photograph by author)

across town to help the young White Sox to a pennant. The team had been created by Charles Comiskey—the Cubs' old foe from Louisville in the 1880s—in 1901 when the American league was born from the rib of the Western League, until then the largest of the minor leagues. Comiskey, eager to gain fan support, claimed the long-abandoned White Stockings name, which soon got shortened to White Sox. Not only were the Remnants one of the NL's only money-losing teams—in sharp contrast to the profitable Sox—but the *Tribune* saw the "old league losing prestige" in the face of the "exciting" upstart that was turning out as "paying venture," arguing that "Chicago fans want a winner and West Side fans want it on the West Side, which is the great baseball center. President Hart is justified in spending money to any reasonable amount to strengthen the next season else the club will become even more of a laughing stock than now."[19]

The next year indeed was a rebuilding one. Incoming manager Frank Selee brought in a large crop of young players, Joe Tinker and Johnny Evers among them. Tinker was a Kansan who had been signed in the spring on a "look-see" basis from the Portland Webfoots, where he could be shipped back if he did not deliver.[20] Evers, from Troy, New York, arrived in Chicago in the fall after making a name for himself playing for his hometown franchise, the same that had birthed the baseball career of fellow Troy native King Kelly. Selee signed him for $100 a month and a $200 purchase price paid to his old club.[21] Tinker and Evers were each twenty-one.

Frank Chance was a relative veteran catcher and right fielder just moved against his wishes to first base by the manager, Selee. Chance, an amateur with no minor league experience, had been signed by Anson in late 1897 after hitting .479 in a California tournament. But in his first five seasons, he had proved an average fielder, had never batted more than .295, and had never played more than seventy-five games in a season. That all would soon change.[22]

The revitalized group was baptized "the Cubs" by the *Chicago Daily News,* and slowly the name began to battle with the others in the press and the hearts of fans.[23] By 1907, as manager, Chance would demand that all media use the name "Cubs" exclusively, as the *Tribune* was still calling them "Spuds" because of the team's Irish American owner Charles Murphy.[24]

THE SADDEST OF
POSSIBLE WORDS?

IN 1903, FOR THE FIRST TIME SINCE 1891, the Cubs finished fewer than ten games off the lead. The very relative resurgence coincided with the first full season to bring together an infield that would become music to fans' ears and go into history as one of the greatest baseball trios and double-play threats of all time: Frank Chance, Johnny Evers, and Joe Tinker.

In 1910, *New York World* columnist Franklin P. Adams would pen "Baseball's Sad Lexicon," one of the most famous baseball pieces ever written:

> These are the saddest of possible words:
> "Tinker to Evers to Chance."
> Trio of bear cubs, and fleeter than birds,
> Tinker and Evers and Chance.
> Ruthlessly pricking our gonfalon bubble,
> Making a Giant hit into a double—
> Words that are heavy with nothing but trouble:
> "Tinker to Evers to Chance."[1]

Over the years, sportswriters and baseball scholars have disputed Tinker, Evers, and Chance's claim on double-play supremacy. Poring over old box scores, New York sportswriter Charlie Segar asserted that "Tinker to Evers to Chance" occurred on average fewer than eight times per season between 1906 and 1909, and "Evers to Tinker to Chance" just more than six times during that span. All in all, according to Segar, the combination accounted for only fifty-six double plays in four years.[2] Many writers have compared the "trio of bear Cubs" unfavorably to latter-day combinations,[3] attempting to knock them off the pedestal they used as a stepping stone to the Hall of Fame (the three Cubs were inducted together in 1946).

Giants manager John McGraw once called a press conference to tell sportswriters, who "have done very well by Tinker, Evers and Chance," that they had "built up a fake, yes a plain fake."[4] Years later, Chicago sportswriter Warren Brown advised: "Don't let anyone tell you the poet's pen isn't mightier than the official scorer's pencil."[5] Jerome Holtzman, the *Chicago Sun-Times* and *Chicago Tribune* writer, who would become Major league Baseball's official historian, dubbed the double-play combination "above average . . . but not much more."[6]

There would be very few chances for the three to turn even one double play their first year together, given their lack of playing time. So his bat could be put to use more often, Chance was converted into a first baseman by new manager Frank Selee in 1902,[7] though Chance appeared only thirty-eight times at the first bag. Evers—a 115-pound, five-foot, nine-inch youngster—was the Orphans' second baseman only eighteen times that year. Tinker—fresh from Portland—established himself at shortstop that year (124 games) after Selee made him switch from third.[8] It would be very late in the season before the first "Tinker to Evers to Chance" on September 15, 1902. Only 260 fans witnessed it.[9]

By 1903, each was a mainstay at the position that would make him famous. Until 1908, they played more than one hundred games each at their positions every year.[10] Chance's early-career injury propensity returned in 1909, when he broke a bone in his shoulder and appeared in just ninety-two games. The total fell to eighty-seven in 1910 and twenty-nine in 1911, when he suffered an ankle injury. The same year, Evers played only thirty-three games at second base and eleven games at third, owing to illness.

Chance, the "Peerless Leader" who had assumed the duties of manager in 1905, took himself out of the lineup in 1912; he played only six times. By 1913 he was gone, along with Tinker. Evers took over as skipper and played most of the season at second base but left the club the following year. By 1914, Tinker-to-Evers-to-Chance was but a memory. That year, Harry Steinfeldt, the third baseman who from 1906 to 1910 had been the "fourth

Tinker, Evers, and Chance (left to right, in 1911) may have been sent to the Hall of Fame as much because of a poem as their baseball. Chance batted .296 and fielded .984 over seventeen major league seasons, and steered the Cubs to a 768-389 record as a manager, winning two World Series and another two NL pennants. Always a hustler, he still holds the Cubs record for stolen bases, with an even four hundred. In addition to being a key part of those teams, Evers won a third World Series title with the Boston Braves, retiring with .270 in batting and .953 in fielding. Tinker batted a more modest .262 and fielded .938 over a fifteen-year career with the Cubs and Chicago Whales. He was, though, a clutch hitter who is the only member of the trio in each of the Cubs' all-time top twenty rankings for hits, doubles, triples, and RBIs. (Library of Congress LC-DIG-bbc-1383f, LC-DIG-bbc-1368f, LC-DIG-bbc-1367f)

leg" of the Cubs infield, died at only thirty-seven years of age. Steinfeldt's star had faded quickly, almost as fast as his health would. After batting a 1907 World Series-best .471, he went 2-for-20 in the 1910 Series and was shipped to St. Paul in the American Association the following spring. His return to the major leagues with the Boston Rustlers was cut short by a mysterious condition that was reported as "nervous prostration" over his being released by the Cubs. After middling attempts at business and a return to baseball, he died in August 1914. The death certificate cited a brain hemorrhage.[11]

In 2002, in his book about Cub greats, Pete Cava penned a postscriptum to Adams's poem that also serves as a belated epitaph for Steinfeldt:

> Here's evidence justice will sometime miscarry,
> "Tinker-to-Evers-to-Chance."
> The Cubs' infield ode fails to mention poor Harry,
> "Tinker-to-Evers-to-Chance."
> Chicago's third baseman, just as sublime,
> As Chance, Evers or Tinker . . . most of the time.
> Left out because Steinfeldt's unwieldy in rhyme,
> "Tinker-to-Evers-to-Chance."[12]

The famous trio's "reign" had really lasted from 1903 to 1910, and the numbers do tell a different tale from the poem. Cubs fans would only mark a 6-4-3 (Tinker-to-Evers-to-Chance) on their score cards twenty-nine times over the span of 1906 through 1909. Even by including Evers-to-Tinker-to-Chance, one only comes up with fifty-four double plays over that four-year period. There were only eight Tinker-to-Evers-to-Chance double plays in 1908, a year when the National League average was seventy-five per team.[13] In four World Series appearances between 1906 and 1910, the Cubs recorded seventeen double plays; not once was it a "Tinker-to-Evers-to-Chance."[14]

After fielding just .972 in 1903, Chance established himself as a premier ball-handler, finishing at or near the top of the league and never fielding less than .989 through the 1911 season. Over at second, Evers's record was more modest. His best year was 1907, when he finished second in the league with .964 in fielding. But he was consistent, and today remains fifth on the Cub's all-time list for second basemen, with a .952 fielding average. He completed the season fourth or lower six times in those eight years. Shortstop Tinker dominated the league three times (1906, '08 and '09) and finished third two more times. He still holds, by far, the franchise record with 574 errors, attenuated by his team record of 3,248 putouts.

The Cubs never finished higher than third in double plays; in the course of eight seasons, their median league ranking for double plays was a modest 4.5. Only once did a Cub lead the league in double plays (Evers, in 1905 with sixty-seven). Still, Evers was in the top half four times, Tinker six times, and Chance two. In comparison, Pittsburgh finished second in 1903–1905 and took the double-play "title" in 1906. Boston then took over as the team giving its pitchers the most consistent defensive assistance, finishing second in double plays in 1906 and '09 and first in 1907, '08, and '10. Boston's eight-year median ranking was second.

One can wonder why Adams did not choose to celebrate Boston's awesome 1910 combination of (former and future Cub) Sweeney to Shean to Sharpe, which not only made for a nice alliteration but also dominated the league (second-bagger Shean was involved in ninety-two double plays, to Chance's forty-eight). Adams was accused of being "a transplanted Chicagoan" (guilty) whose "habit" it was "to root against the Giants."[15] Beyond his alleged sweet spot for anything Chicagoan, the writer in him may have been lured by using surnames—Tinker and Chance, and to a lesser degree, Evers—loaded with symbolism.

What perhaps best distinguished the Cubs trio is that it had managed to stay together. In its four years at or near the top of the league, Pittsburgh went through three different double-play combinations. Boston's combination changed every year from 1906 to 1910. Sweeney, Shean, and Sharpe had their gloves on their side, but not familiarity. Nor did they win World Series and record exploits with their bats in the process.[16]

The Chicago trio also made contributions to baseball folklore that did not involve balls, bats, or gloves—save for boxing gloves. On April 16, 1906, Evers and Chance got the boot for their on-field antics and Tinker got in a fight with a fan.[17] Evers was often sent packing by umpires for various outbursts. In the July 8, 1907 game, Chance hurled bottles back at Brooklyn fans after the supporters pelted him with them. He hit a young boy and had to leave under police escort before serving a suspension.[18]

Chance's feisty attitude was, for one, an extension of his win-at-all-costs playing style. New York Giants pitcher Christy Mathewson described it: "If he has to choose between accepting a pair of spikes in a vital part of his anatomy and getting a put-out, or dodging the spikes and losing the put-out, he always takes the put-out and usually the spikes."[19] Chance was so aggressive at the plate that he was hit by a pitch a franchise-leading 137 times (for perspective, the second Cub on the list is Ernie banks with seventy). The repeated beanings were a contributor to his retirement as a player. On July 1, 1911, he collapsed during a game owing to a blood clot. He experienced headaches and deafness after that and doctors were reported to fear another blow could prove fatal. Chance was so often hit by pitches that Hugh Fullerton used his photograph to illustrate the entry for "bean" in his "Baseball Primer," noting that Chance had had to give up playing because he had been beaned so many times.[20]

Much has been written about the fact Tinker and Evers did not speak for years after a fistfight, though the spat did not last as long as many historians thought. Gil Bogen, who wrote a joint biography of the three men, places the triggering event in 1905, with Tinker and Evers years after the fact agreeing only on the fistfight, but giving different reasons for it. "He threw me a hard ball. . . . it broke my finger . . . we fought and agreed to stop talking," Evers recollected. Tinker, for his part, remembered, "Evers got in a hack [taxi] all by himself and drove off . . . I was mad . . . we were at it, rolling among the bats on the ball field. . . . You play your position and I'll play mine and let it go at that."[21] By 1908, the pair was speaking, but had yet to shake hands. Bogen also revisited an emotional reunion in 1924, brought about by Chance as he was dying in California.[22]

It also did not hurt that Chance was a master player-manager. After his average first few years with the team, Chance was transformed when he moved to first base. He batted .310 or better each year from 1903 through 1906. By 1910, when Adams wrote the poem, Chance's Cubs had bested Ty Cobb and the Tigers twice in the World Series, and he had compiled one of the most formidable managing runs of all time. From 1906 through 1909, under the "Peerless Leader," the Cubs averaged 106 wins per year. Over the five years from 1906 until 1910, they finished first four times, their worst season being second in 1909. Of the seven full seasons Chance would manage the Cubs, their worst showing would be ninety-one wins. Evers was in such awe of Chance's skills as a manager that in *Touching Second* in early 1910, he reprinted and amended a riveting article from *The American Magazine*:

> Suddenly, at the end of the tense line of athletes on the bench there was a movement. A player with earnest, but rather weary face, immobile even in the moment when the whole result of his year's work might be ruined, raised his right hand to his cap, lifted it an inch from his head, replaced it and without a muscle of his face twitching sat watching.
>
> Like a flash the coacher at third base sprang down the line. "Look out, Steiny," he screamed. "Look out, Frank," came the echo from the first

A catcher turned first baseman, Frank Chance was not above getting into fights with players and still leads the Cubs' all-time list for players hit by pitches, umpires, and opposing fans. As player-manager he steered the Cubs to a 530-235 record over 1906–1910 and batted .421 in the 1908 World Series. (Library of Congress LC-USZ62-133648)

base coacher's box. The pitcher wound himself into fantastic contortions. From somewhere out of the tangle of revolving limbs a ball shot like a flash to the plate, into the catcher's mitt. As the pitcher started to wind up, the runner at first base leaped twenty feet towards second, stopped, hesitated, and took a step back towards first base. The catcher, who had caught the ball in perfect position, leaped forward, right arm drawn back, watchful, alert, in perfect position to throw to second base. The crowd groaned. Another strike on the batter; the effort to steal balked. Slowly the catcher relaxed from his tense poise. His arm dropped and he started to throw the ball easily back to the pitcher. In that instant the runner at first base was galvanized into action. Two tremendous leaps toward second, and he was flying at full speed down the line. The catcher hesitating a trice, tightened again into throwing position, and threw like a rifle shot to second just as he caught a glimpse of a figure tearing homeward from third. An instant later, in a whirling cloud of dust, a runner pivoted around the plate, his foot dragging across the rubber just as the ball, hastily hurled back to the catcher, came down upon his leg. The umpire's hands went down. The run had scored. The game was won. The crowd in a tumult of enthusiasm roared and screamed and shrilled its joy. The man at the end of the bench let a shadow of a smile flit over his face, and watched more intently than ever. The crowd had forgotten him, and was cheering the others. Let us see what really happened, for the play described is the one by which Frank Chance saved the championship of 1908 by beating New York one game on the West Side grounds. The crowd saw everything—that is, everything it could see. What it did not see was this: Tinker was batting, Steinfeldt was on first base, Schulte on third. The orders were for a hit and run play when Tinker went to bat. After one strike had been called Chance raised his hand, lifted his cap from his head and quickly replaced it; the signal for his men to attempt a delayed double steal. Marshall, coaching at third cried: "Look out, Steiny," and Evers, coaching at first, "Look out, Frank." No one noticed in the jumble of their yells, that they used the names of the base runners for the first time. The use of the name of a runner was the signal for the delayed double steal. All that happened afterwards was only mechanical, and although Schulte scored, and Steinfeldt reached second and Tinker helped them by his motions as he struck at the ball, intentionally missing it, they were but puppets carrying out the orders of the general. Chance had won the game from the bench when he lifted his cap from his head.[23]

Chance and his fellow Cubs were adept at stealing bases. Chance stole four hundred over his career, the most ever by a Cub. Tinker and Evers swiped 304 and 291, respectively, good for fifth and sixth most all-time for the team. But, likely out of a combination of skill and tireless practice, the Cubs did not always need the signs, for steals or anything else. The *Chicago*

Tribune's Hugh Fullerton would recall, "I have seen the Chicago Cubs play entire series without a sign being used, when this elaborate system of secret signals was unnecessary as each man knew what to do."[24]

Tinker and Evers too would try their hand at managing in later years. Tinker kept on playing for the Cubs through 1912, when a contract dispute led him to take the assignment of player-manager for the Cincinnati Reds. His best season as a player came with that team in 1913, when he posted career-high numbers in batting (.317) and fielding (a still-modest .968), but the team finished 37½ games off the pace. Tinker managed and played two years in Chicago for the Federal League's Whales, winning the pennant in the rival league by .001 in 1915. Fittingly, he played his last seven games with the Cubs in 1916, the year he managed his old club to a fifth-place finish, 26½ games behind. After that, he had a spotty business career in Florida. He, like Anson before, went into the billiards business, but real estate was the mainstay; he went from being a millionaire to destitute at the time of his 1948 death, following a leg amputation and uncontrolled diabetes.[25] Tinker always stayed active in baseball, mostly as a scout, and Tinker Field in Orlando was dedicated in his honor in 1923.[26]

Evers was player-manager for the Cubs in 1913, good for a third-place finish but not good enough for owner Charles Murphy, who announced Evers's resignation as manager before the 1914 season, prompting Evers to deny he had quit and to expose the true situation: a contract and salary dispute. He had, in effect, been locked out. Evers was traded after the National League intervened to avoid losing another star to the Federal League. He took over second base, but not the managerial duties, for Boston and helped the Braves win the 1914 World Series. That year, Evers was named the NL's Most Valuable Player, while the Cubs finished fourth and 16½ games behind under umpire-turned-manager Hank O'Day.[27] Evers played through 1917.

Turned away at the army recruiting office because of his age, Evers still served in World War I in France, as the Knights of Columbus athletic director for U.S. servicemen in Europe. Years later, he recounted organizing a game at Verdun while the cannons went about their business just three miles away.[28]

He returned briefly to the Cubs as a manager in 1921, when the team finished seventh with a paltry .416 winning percentage. Evers's 1924

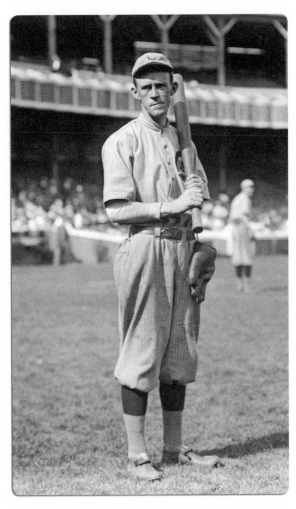

Somewhat overshadowed by the achievements of player-manager Frank Chance, Johnny Evers was one of the mainstays of the era. Most of his career was spent with the Cubs beginning in 1902, but he was dismissed after a dispute with management in 1913. He left the team to anchor World Series–winning Boston in 1914. Shown here in 1910, he died in 1947 after several strokes and under the strain of financial hardship. (Library of Congress LC-DIG-ggbain-08323)

engagement with the White Sox ended with an eighth-place finish, 25½ games off first, but it was crowned by a playing tour in England before King George V.[29]

Chance was set to take over the Chicago White Sox from Evers in 1924, when illness struck and he had to return home. A combination of heart trouble and asthma would kill him in California that September. Unlike the other two members of the trio, he would die very well off thanks to his part ownership in the Cubs. He left an estate worth $250,000 (nearly $3.5 million in 2014 dollars).[30]

The rest of Evers's life was spent focused on the family sporting goods store in Albany, New York, another brief stint as assistant manager for the Braves, and various scouting assignments and minor-league front office positions. The Great Depression was rough on his business and finances, and by 1936 he was bankrupt. Evers was given a job as superintendent of a small stadium in Albany and continued to work at his store. The last of several strokes killed him in 1947.[31] When Tinker, Evers, and Chance were inducted into the Hall of Fame in 1946, Evers, bed-ridden, said, "I'm glad we made it all together."[32]

"THE FELLOWS WHO MADE THE GAME"

ADJECTIVES IN EARLY BASEBALL COVERAGE were almost as rare as an unassisted triple play. Chicago newspaper writers soon began giving readers more vivid and lively accounts of games with what has been called the Chicago style of baseball reporting. Slang, metaphor, and simile crept into the sports pages on their way to the rest of the paper and the language.[1] This not only helped change how the papers covered everything else, but it expanded the reach of baseball across Chicago through the "new idea in making the reports of the games interesting and entertaining enough to be read by all patrons of the paper. . . . Readers, laughing at the accounts of games and the doings of the players, commenced to go to see for themselves. The style of reporting baseball changed all over the country." Editors did not encourage this solely for love of the game; circulation also rose.[2]

A generation of Chicago newsmen in particular has been credited with helping to break from the drabness of early baseball coverage. These young or reform-minded writers broke away from the press establishment by starting their own club in 1889, partly because they rejected their peers' compliance with what they perceived as the corrupt social order, and partly because they could not afford the dues of the leading clubs, given their meager salaries. Those of them who covered baseball typically saw the world from the players' standpoint—with whom they more or less lived on the road—and naturally gravitated toward the gritty, rebellious aspect of the game, compared to the self-aggrandizing, staid baseball rhetoric

ALWAYS FIRST ON THE STREET.

In the late 1880s, the *Chicago Daily News* prided itself in reporting the game almost in real time through the groundbreaking use of the telephone. The evening paper came out with an account of that afternoon's game. (Author's collection)

adopted for so long by the likes of Spalding and Anson. For years they had banded together while covering stories over the 1880s, a decade during which Chicago counted as many as ten different local newspapers. The formalized grouping called itself the Whitechapel Club, and its leader was a reporter for the *Chicago Record Herald,* Charles Seymour. It also included such members as cub reporters Finley Peter Dunne and George Ade.[3]

Dunne was a reporter at several Chicago papers beginning in the mid-1880s and later the man behind the Mr. Dooley cartoons and such books as *Mr. Dooley's Opinions*. Though he and Seymour did take a new, colorful approach to covering the game, reports of their seminal contributions may have been exaggerated. Dunne's biographer, Elmer Ellis, described the two men as constant companions who helped change sports journalism when the Chicago papers decided to step up their coverage in 1887 following the 1885 and 1886 pennant wins by the White Stockings. Before them, Elmer wrote, baseball news amounted to little more than just printing the results or just box scores, and several books since then have repeated the claim.[4] As Dunne's various biographers would have it, he changed baseball writing almost overnight. In truth, the process was underway when he entered the business, though he definitely was a creative force in the movement.

Ellis, for example, traces the origin of the word "southpaw" to the Cubs and credits Dunne and Seymour with coining the term in 1887 because, at West Side Park, home plate was on the west end and a left-handed pitcher's throwing arm would have been to the south. He stresses that the term appeared only in their stories in Chicago papers that year, and that the term was not listed in 1888's *The Krank, His Language and What it Means*, by Thomas Lawson.[5] Others have promulgated the Ellis story, among other possibilities, as to the origin of the phrase in a baseball and a pitching context.[6] In fact, the term appeared as early as 1848 in a boxing context and in 1876 in a baseball position player context, long before West Side Park existed.[7] In January 1885, the Philadelphia-based *Sporting Life* was describing a pitcher as a southpaw, six months after Dunne graduated high school and two years before he was covering baseball at the tender age of twenty.[8]

Early baseball reporting could undeniably be bland. On October 23, 1876, the *Inter Ocean* marked the end of the home team's pennant-winning season under the small headline "Base Ball" with this report on page 3, followed by the names of the expected '77 team, without any mention of their prior affiliation:

A special dispatch from Milwaukee conveys to base-ball enthusiasts the pleasing intelligence that the Whites had scooped up the last game of the season. The encounter was a very interesting one, as the score below will show. This is probably the last game the home team of '76 will play together again. [Next year's team] comprise what is possibly the strongest nine ever made up.

The uninspired style may have owed to the fact that the teams themselves sometimes provided copy to the papers. Tom Foley of the early White Stockings is reported to have done so, and it is not unlikely this continued for some time. This may explain the boast in the story above, which may have been more awkward infomercial than article.[9] By 1880, the coverage remained laconic but did include more of the happenings on the field. Here is the entire article by "special telegram to the *Inter Ocean*" about a 3–1 victory by the White Stockings:

> The game to-day was a contest of pitchers, Corcoran proving himself the better man. The Chicagos made all their runs in the eighth inning on a two-base hit by Darlymple, singles by Gore and Kelly, sacrifice hits by Williamson and Corcoran, and an error by Craemer. The Worcesters made their only run on a base on balls, passed ball and wild throw by Flint. The attendance was 497.[10]

Around that time, the innovation in Chicago papers came more on the statistical rather than the stylistic front, giving readers a better ability to gauge player performance. In 1876, the *Chicago Times* began calculating fielding based on chances rather than games played.[11]

Soon, however, there was some groundbreaking baseball coverage in Chicago papers, especially the *Daily Inter Ocean,* some years before Dunne and Seymour got involved, though coverage overall was still very mixed. This excerpt from an 1882 article is an example of the better writing earlier in the decade in the *Chicago Herald,* with a more vivid account of some plays:

> [Pitcher Larry] Corcoran surprised everyone, and, no doubt, himself, by making a home run, two two-base hits, one single, two runs and pitching a wonderful game. . . . The prettiest fielding play of the year was made by Nicol in right field, making a running stop of a difficult grounder from Evans' bat and throwing fairly to first base, putting out the batter by a hair's breadth.[12]

In 1883, the *Inter Ocean* was sprinkling some color in its inning-by-inning reports:

> The game was supposed to be remarkable from the fact that Cleveland would present a phenomenal pitcher in the person of Sawyer. When this

gentleman entered the box everyone was prepared to see the Chicagos retire in rotation, but, strange to say, the home nine knocked the phenomenon "higher than a kite," and came very close to whitewashing the visitors by the most excellent field playing of the season.[13]

These separate articles from 1885, from the *Inter Ocean* and *Tribune,* respectively, show further evolution:

A rather shabby attempt to beat the Chicagos out of a run was made by Donnelly, who stuck his foot out to trip McCauley, who was running to third base. McCauley saw the foot in time to jump over it, but the action brought out the hisses of the crowd.[14]

Gore had run up from center, but his wild reach for the ball was ineffectual, and Darlymple having failed to back up Gore in his effort, the ball went bounding off toward the carriages. Dal finally secured it, however, and threw to Pfeffer at second. The latter made a wild pass at the ball as it flew by his ear, and before Anson could capture it, both Ward and Gillespie had crossed the home plate amidst the plaudits of the spectators. ... Dorgan, in right field, also made a great catch of Pfeffer's fly, as did Darlymple of Connor's sky-scraper to left.[15]

On October 6, 1886, with the home team in the thick of its second pennant race in two years—it had only a two-game lead—the *Chicago Daily News'* sports "section" was a seven-paragraph messy affair that jumped back and forth from horse races to unrelated baseball items. When it did get to the account of the White Stockings' game, it did not mince words:

A New York dispatch speaking of yesterdays' ball game says that, judging from the actions of several of the Chicago players before and after the game, they seemed to be utterly indifferent as to the result. Gore misjudged one fly and muffed another; Williamson played carelessly and allowed a run to come in; Flynn pitched poorly and was badly supported by Hardie.

The editors of the *Daily News,* who had resisted sports coverage but had to know they were falling behind other papers in the vivaciousness of the stories at a time when the city was going baseball crazy, decided to give more prominent play to the 1886 championship games against St. Louis, though the results were spotty and it is unclear who was doing the reporting. October 18, 1886 marked the first game of the series between Chicago and the Browns after the White Stockings snatched the National League pennant by 2½ games. The next day, to find an account of it in the *Daily News,* readers would have had to direct their attention to the bottom right corner of the front page, where a brief article appeared under a small-type headline that read, "sporting affairs." After news of horse racing and billiards, this grabber appeared in the fourth paragraph: "Chicagos, 6; St. Louis, 0. The first game of the world's championship series was decided yesterday by the above score." The rest of the article does give more detail and displays more wit than Elmer would have us believe, and it even includes a rare direct quote by a player. But it does beg for more color and description of some plays:

> The Browns played all the ball they knew but were simply outclassed by the champions of the league. Latham, the clown of the diamond, used every means within his power to rattle the White Stockings, but his words had no more effect than if he talked to a brick wall. The Chicagos went in to win, and as the "only Kelly" expressed himself: "We wanted to see how hard they would make us play. We'll do 'em for the series, too."[16]

Four days later, as St. Louis took the lead in the series, the evening *Daily News* splashed a large headline at the top of its front page, "St Louis Wins," with one of several subheads reading, "Many Brilliant Plays by the Garden City Delegates." However, if brilliance there was, it did not come across in the long, linear article, which does have the virtue of relaying exactly what took place, though only through the first five innings: owing no doubt to print-press deadlines, the narrative ended there, supplemented by a box score that only went through six innings and then listed the final score of St. Louis 10, Chicago 3, the first time the score was mentioned at all. Here is a sample:

> Fifth Inning—For Chicago Kelly hit safe to Gleason. Anson's fly was captured by Carruthers. Kelly stole second and went to third on Pfeffer's sacrifice hit to Comiskey. Williamson went to first on balls and stole second. Burns went out from short to second, leaving Kelly and Williamson on bases.[17]

The next day, the Browns wrapped it up, and the *Daily News* ran a story with the same placement under a large headline that declared "St. Louis Crazy" and subheads that proclaimed "the Brown-Stockings win the sixth game and the Championship of the World" and "Chicago ball-tossers clearly outclassed." Here was the lead:

> When Capt. Anson with his aggregation of ball-players came on the field this afternoon he was greeted by a crowd which was probably smaller than those which have greeted him for the past two days. The sky was cloudy and clear by turns and kept the audience guessing as to whether it would rain or not.[18]

By 1887, with Dunne now reporting, the reading experience was markedly improved. Prominent front-page treatment was less rare, even during earlier parts of the season. The August 2, 1887 lead, for example, was a radical departure from the previous year: "The senators were wonderfully surprised yesterday at the idea of coming to Chicago and losing the first game, for it had never crossed their befuddled brains before." Earlier in the summer, on July 21, an on-field dispute during an away game against Boston received this treatment: "The discussion was loud and pointed. But shortly before the umpire was talked to death, he declared Baldwin out and saved his life. Anson refused to submit and kept on talking. The crowd cheered, hissed, and called out 'Play ball.' Finally the Chicagos went to the field." On September 5, Dunne wrote a rare preview of the day's game, an account of the team's trip to Detroit from Washington and of a conversation between Anson and the umpire, who had gotten on board the same train as the White Stockings at Niagara. Dunne quoted the umpire mentioning the possibility that the White Stockings, who were a distant second to Detroit, might in fact finish second. He then printed Anson's indignant reaction, describing him as "becoming as red in the face as a baby chocking on popcorn."

In the August 8, 1887 *Daily News,* Dunne re-created the palpable excitement of a Billy Sunday catch the day before:

> The bravest feat performed in many a day was the phenomenal catch of Tiernan's long fly by Right Fielder Sunday in Saturday's Game. The people opened a gap and with a tremendous leap he cleared the bench, his speed carrying him against the brick wall with great force. Ten thousand

pairs of eyes saw him throw his arms above his head, and they were ready to applaud the act, but no one expected that he had caught the ball. As he turned and limped away from the wall, holding aloft the ball for judgment, the shouts of the crowd could be heard for blocks away.[19]

Years later, Dunne, no doubt informed by his time with the White Stockings and his own shortcomings as a student—he finished last in his high school class of fifty—had Mr. Dooley say, "Fractions druv him fr'm school, an' th' vagrancy laws druv him to baseball."[20]

Over at the *Chicago Herald*, Seymour had editors who, unlike Dunne's, did not insist on the proper usage of the Queen's English. His account of a July 16, 1887 Chicago victory over New York opened with a lead that had the flavor of Dunne's latter-years Mr. Dooley, albeit with a New York twist:

> "Dere's jist dis about it," said a freckled-faced West Ender in a pink shirt as he spread a handkerchief on the bleaching boards at the Polo Grounds this afternoon and then sat down on it. "Dere's jist dis about it. Anson is the only bloke on dis ball of dirt dat can run a base ball club as she oughter to be run, see? And say, he can come down here and make monkeys of dese 'joints' just as often as he wants ter. Yez may talk all yez amind to, but Anson is de cuckoo of da hull lot. Dere's no herring about him, ace."[21]

Dunne and Seymour were not alone in reshaping their craft. In fact, above all others, Hugh Fullerton praised another young reporter, Leonard Washburn, who wrote for the *Inter Ocean* from 1887 until his death in a train wreck in Crete, Illinois, in 1891. Fullerton credited Washburn's enterprising editors, who before those at papers like the *Daily News,* permitted Washburn "to lift baseball out of the literary class of the market reports." Washburn won over readers with this description of a Ned Williamson ground ball on an ill-mowed infield: it went toward short "sounding like the hired man eating celery." There was, Fullerton noted, a drawback to having such bon vivants covering the game: "If the reporters and athletes met after a game the chances of the reporters getting back to write their reports were not good."[22]

The *Daily News,* which had an evening edition, devised a way around this challenge that was, more than reporting style, the paper's true innovation: immediacy. To wow readers, it took them behind the curtain to show how it had revolutionized coverage and, no doubt, to show up the competition on

The *Daily News'* observation post on the roof of the grandstands at West Side Grounds. (Author's collection)

the day of the last home game of the 1887 season. To avoid seeing "admirers of the home team tossed on uneasy beds at night, waiting for the morning papers," the *Daily News* had installed a "cross between a dry goods case and a patrol box" on top of the grandstands, where one man observed the action and the other stood in the back on a telephone, "instantaneously reporting a game of baseball." The secret of the speed, the paper breathlessly explained, was a special telephone line back to the newspaper, faster than the previously used telegraph wires. At the newspaper office, a man's ear was glued to the phone, repeating every word to a typist who, after each inning, handed his sheet to a messenger boy who ran it to press. Late finishes precluded accounts of the last few innings to be printed. No matter, alert pressmen stood by the phone and added the lead to the laid-out box score to include the tallies of the last innings, and started the press. The first sheets were folded and grabbed by a boy who "though he possesses no wings . . . fairly flies out and a crowd of men standing on the sidewalk and waiting for him to grab his papers as though they were the last on earth. And how long do you think it has been since that last player went out on four strikes till the gentleman with the cutaway coat and the bandy legs got his paper and started to read it? Well, it may have been thirty seconds, but it was not more." Within five minutes of the end of the contest, boys were "running in every direction on the west, north and south sides with big bundles of papers," the early version of "sports final." The same article revealed, unwittingly, another secret: Dunne was fabricating most of the action. His "watcher" would say, "Anson: home run—Congress street." And then Dunne would "fashion" it into this prose, dictated into the phone without having seen the play: "Then Capt. Anson, with a mighty lunge, hurled his bat against an out-curve and the ball rose in a slightly parabola and, describing Hogarth's line of beauty, descended upon the Congress street wall." And so it turns out, Dunne was not quite a baseball writer but one of baseball's first announcers, what the *Daily News* euphemistically called "the baseball artist."[23]

By the end of the decade, the livelier style spilled over from the stories and spiced up headlines. When it reported that Frank Flint, a catcher with the White Stockings from 1879 to 1889, was dying of consumption, the *Chicago Times'* headline announced he was "Nearing the home plate."[24] A week later, after the inevitable had happened, the paper used the headline, "Gets his final release" with a subhead that read, "Crosses eternal home plate."[25]

George Ade, another member of the Whitechapel Club, had a similarly witty take on baseball and death. A reporter for the *Chicago Record,* he soon expanded to short stories for the newspaper, a practice that future Chicago writers like Ring Lardner would take to new heights. Here is Ade's "The Fable of the Base Ball Fan Who Took the Only Cure:"

ONCE upon a Time a Base Ball
Fan lay on his Death-Bed.
He had been a Rooter from
the days of Underhand Pitching.

It was simply Pie for him to tell in what year Anse began to play with the Rockfords and what Kelly's Batting Average was the Year he sold for Ten Thousand.

If you asked him who played Center for Boston in 1886 he could tell you quick—right off the Reel. And he was a walking Directory of all the Glass. Arms in the Universe.

More than once he had let drive with a Pop Bottle at the Umpire and then yelled "Robber" until his Pipes gave out. For many Summers he would come Home, one Evening after Another, with his Collar melted, and tell his Wife that the Giants made the Colts look like a lot of Colonial Dames playing Bean Bag in a Weedy Lot back of an Orphan Asylum, and they ought to put a Trained Nurse on Third, and the Dummy at Right needed an Automobile, and the New Man couldn't jump out of a Boat and hit the Water, and the Short-Stop wouldn't be able to pick up a Ball if it was handed to him on a Platter with Water Cress around it, and the Easy One to Third that ought to have been Sponge Cake was fielded like a One-Legged Man with St. Vitus dance trying to do the Nashville Salute.

Of course she never knew what he was Talking about, but she put up with it, Year after Year, mixing Throat Gargle for him and reading the Games to him when he was having his Eyes tested and had to wear a Green Shade.

At last he came to his Ninth Inning and there were Two Strikes called and no Balls, and his Friends knew it was All Day with him. They stood around and tried to forget that he was a Fan. His Wife wept softly and consoled herself with the Thought that possibly he would have amounted to Something if there had been no National Game. She forgave Everything and pleaded for one Final Message. His Lips moved. She leaned over and Listened. He wanted to know if there was Anything in the Morning Papers about the Condition of Bill Lange's Knee.[26]

The second generation of the Chicago cohort was ushered in by Charles Dryden, who Fullerton dubbed "The Mark Twain of baseball." Offered the baseball beat by Dunne, now editor, he chronicled, among other feats, the 1906 Cubs-Sox series for the *Tribune.* Another key figure was Hugh Fullerton himself, who covered baseball and other sports for the *Tribune* and became the patrician of the Chicago press corps. He helped found the Baseball Writers Association of America, and immortalized his predecessors and peers in the *Saturday Evening Post* in 1928, recording their influence on the growth of baseball in a lengthy piece titled, "The Fellows Who Made the Game," quoted at the outset of this chapter.[27] He also coauthored Johnny Evers's baseball book, *Touching Second*.

Though Fullerton stands on his own as a reporter, one of his greatest contributions may have been bringing one Ring Lardner to the *Tribune*.[28] Lardner would cover the Cubs and White Sox, and after a few years take over Fullerton's "In the Wake of the News" column in 1914 until he left Chicago in 1919. His true fame came from his short stories, the first of which featured a character he had made up, like Dunne before. The antihero was Jack Keefe, a semiliterate player whom audiences first met in 1914 in the *Saturday Evening Post* in a story called, "A Busher's Letter Home," which chronicled Jack's early days on the White Sox through notes to a friend back home.[29] Lardner's most enduring legacy as far as Cubs fans are concerned is that he orchestrated and promoted the Cubs' first barbershop quartet, which likely played a part in popularizing "Take Me Out to the Ball Game" in Chicago after the song was published in 1908 and spread through such musical groups.[30]

Sometimes, the writers even became the story. In 1906, Fullerton wrote a piece predicting a Sox win before the Cubs-Sox World Series began or, as he called it, the Spuds-Sox series. Editors, or more likely perhaps someone in management, held the story, for fear of ridicule and disrepute for the *Tribune* should the prediction prove wrong. On October 15, 1906 the paper, in the midst of its four pages of coverage on the Sox victory, ran his original story under the headline, "Series Verifies Fullerton's Dope," with an introduction about the prediction having been withheld by "a man in authority." Other subheads proclaimed "Tribune Expert Forecasts Exact Result Before the Contests Begin . . . Tell How He Did It . . . Prophecy, Suppressed After Being Prepared, is Founded on Figures." The story did not reveal how upset Fullerton must have been to have been denied the pride of having run the piece before the first inning of the first game.

He, Dryden, and Lardner were famous in their own right, but Fullerton, reflecting in 1928, concluded, "somehow the pioneer writers got more of the atmosphere of the game, more of the scent of the dugout."[31]

OUT IN LEFT FIELD?

AS SPORTSWRITERS BECAME MORE CREATIVE, more and more of the game's colorful imagery permeated everyday English in a way achieved by no other American sport. One prominent expression may even have been born at Cubs park. From the clutch hitter who bats a thousand to the pinch hitter who came to play ball and is ready to go to bat for his teammate, the shadow of the ballplayer is present in descriptions of other sports and work situations. "It is interesting to note the number of metaphors that arise out of the teamwork aspect of baseball, and how few arise from the competitive nature of the game," commented Maggie Sokolik at a symposium on the sport. "We can see, through this idealization of baseball, that we value self-sacrifice, cooperation, and teamwork above individual accomplishment and stardom."

This is not to say that society does not recognize those who make it out of the bush leagues and into the big leagues. In the United States, at least, human interaction is also loaded with baseball lingo, as one person will throw a curveball to another, who might choose either to play hardball or field the question. And high school students may once have touched base with each other or ended up getting to first base. Decision makers who give ballpark figures at meetings may turn out to be off-base. Thus, Sokolik concludes, "baseball structures our time, space, interpersonal relationships, and standards of accomplishment."[1]

Had University of Chicago Professor William McClintock had his way in the 1910s, the English language would have been rid forever of these insidious baseball idioms. He was rebuffed with calls that "the slang of today is the purest English tomorrow" in the press, which itself was primarily responsible for the changes he was decrying: "The injury which is now proposed is the abolition of the language of baseball. This, as all the world knows, is a distinctive and peculiar tongue. It is not English. It is not precisely slang. It is a strange patois, full of idiomatic eccentricities, rich in catch phrases and technical terms, wonderfully expressive and in the highest degree flexible."[2]

In Chicago, that patois was taking hold. There are mentions in the literature, and an urban legend, of Chicago's West Side Grounds being the birthplace of the idiom "out in left field." There is strong evidence to support this theory, but this is no home run.

William Safire defined the expression as "out of contact with reality," which was not to be confused with "out of left field," which merely meant farfetched.[3] Safire made a seminal mention of the possible link between West Side Grounds and "out in left field" in his 1984 *I Stand Corrected*, one that Christine Ammer's 1993 *Southpaws and Sunday Punches* and Paul Dickson's 2009 *Dickson Baseball Dictionary* picked up. Among several theories about the origins of the phrase, the Chicago version is perhaps the most convincing, though not for the exact reasons listed in those books.

Beginning in 1891 and well after the Cubs left for the North Side, Cook County housed "all persons suspected of insanity, who come under police control, and those for whom a petition for a hearing in lunacy is made" and "feeble-minded children" at the Cook County Detention Hospital at the northwest corner of Wood and Polk Streets—across the street from the Cubs' ballpark. The Detention Hospital overlooked left field. By the early 1910s, it was replaced with the Cook County Psychopathic Hospital, designed for "the actual care of patients who have been unfortunate enough to break down mentally." The new structure was five-stories high along Wood and part of Polk. The upper floors were made up of wards and patient rooms that fronted the street and had many windows, supporting uncorroborated modern tales that inmates' screams could be heard from the ballpark.[4]

These facts alone back up the theory. But it is through more tenuous, circuitous means that the theory first found its way into the literature. Dickson cites as evidence a letter from a Chicago physician, Gerald M. Eisenberg, M.D., published in William Safire's *I Stand Corrected:* "In Chicago, when someone said that one was 'out in left field,' the implication was that one was

The University of Illinois' Medical Campus (buildings labeled 1 through 9) occupied much of the old West Side Grounds site by the mid 1930s. The Cook County Psychopathic Hospital is labeled number 12. (University Archives Photo Collection, [LHS-UA-88-002-0698], University of Illinois at Chicago Library of the Health Sciences, Special Collections)

behaving like the occupants of the Neuropsychiatric Institute, which was literally out in left field." [5] Ammer used the same language without sourcing it. [6] In his book, Safire, true to his policy that whether one is a "Language Snob" or a "Language Slob" [7] is in the eye of the beholder, did not really pick one side in the debate over where "out in left field" comes from. But it is instructive to read the entire letter, rather than the brief snippet quoted by Dickson.

Though Dickson never states it, the entry could create in some readers the impression that the letter's author has first-hand knowledge of the matter. It is clear, however, given the full letter's various inaccuracies, that the author had no direct knowledge of the ballpark:

The original Cubs ballpark was located at the corner of Wood and Polk streets on Chicago's Near West Side.

In fact, the ballpark was called West Side Ballpark. The site is now occupied by the University of Illinois College of Medicine, and has been since the 1920s.

Home plate was located on the corner of Wood and Polk, and left field was located down Wood Street. Immediately behind the left field stands was located (and still is) the Neuropsychiatric Institute, which is now part of the University.

In Chicago, when someone said that one was "out in left field," the implication was that one was behaving like the occupants of the Neuropsychiatric Institute, which was literally out in left field.

After West Side ballpark was torn down, it was a number of years before the remainder of the medical school was built, and ball games on the vacant land still took place. It didn't take long before the phrase "out in left field" became commonplace to describe someone who was acting like they were "nuts."

Eisenberg, who still practices in the Chicago area, confirmed he had never been to the ballpark; no one had bothered to ask. He completed his internship, residency, and fellowship at the University of Illinois and Cook County hospitals from the mid-1970s to the early 1980s, almost on top of the old ballpark. The letter captured the stories told by his elders. "At the time, these were already World War II guys," he said.[8]

By the time it got to Eisenberg, the story was two generations removed from the team's years at West Side Grounds. Eisenberg played a pivotal role in this etymological mystery when he committed the tale to paper, preserving it for future exploration. Like a lot of oral history, the tale got a lot of the details wrong but preserved the essential gist, which allowed subsequent research and confirmation of the actual facts.

For the record, the name of the ballpark was West Side Grounds, not West Side Ballpark; home plate was a ways away from Polk along Lincoln (Wolcott), not at Polk and Wood; and the Neuropsychiatric Institute did not exist at the time of the ballpark, though the Detention Hospital and the Psychopathic Hospital did. The institute was not absorbed by the university, rather it was built as part of it after the ballpark was gone. It did not have "occupants," but the Cook County institution did.

One implication from Eisenberg's story could be that the ballpark came first (and went) and the saying originated after the ballpark was destroyed. In this version, Chicagoans (be they, as Eisenberg writes, participants in pick-up games on the site, or simply visitors to the new University of Illinois hospital and College of Medicine facilities, or anyone who had been to the ballpark) coined "out in left field" because there now was a mental health facility near where left field used to be. Given that construction was not completed until 1941 and the institute did not open until 1942, this sequencing would mean the Chicago use of the idiom would have come after the earliest use of the phrase in 1937, though in that instance it was used to describe an odd-ball of a wisecracking baseball player named Lefty Gomez.[9] It is likely the presence of the newer Neuropsychiatric Institute, which sits in the old left centerfield at 950 South Wood Street, just created confusion and that those repeating the story over the decades simply got the name of the mental institution wrong.

To the claim that baseball games would have been staged on the site for some years, it is improbable, though not impossible, given the sequencing of construction on the site. The University of Illinois purchased the site in 1919, and the ballpark was torn down in 1920. The first wave of construction for the University of Illinois College of Medicine ended in 1925, covering the old home plate, infield, part of left field, and the north grandstand. Construction continued through the 1930s throughout the site. In the early 1940s, the Neuropsychiatric Institute was erected over left center. It would be 1954 before the rest of the old left field was gobbled up by the Clinical Sciences Building (CSB). With so much construction and shrinking vacant land, no full-scale games could have been staged, but pick-up games certainly would have been possible, given that most of center and left field was left open for about three decades.[10] A more likely revised theory is that the expression stems from West Side Grounds because the mental institution was just beyond the left field wall.

The other main theory on the origin of the phrase is also mentioned by Dickson and based on a fan's letter in the same William Safire book.[11] That fan, David Shulman, wrote about being a Bronx resident who went to Yankees games as a teen, when "out in left field" was directed at Yankees

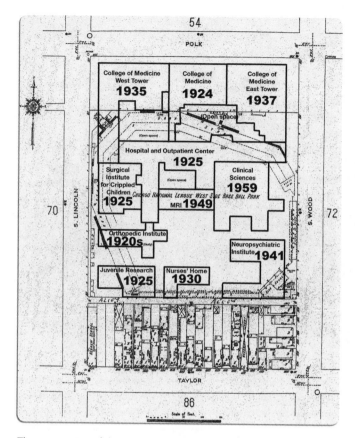

The sequencing of the construction of the University of Illinois College of Medicine and related buildings is shown here superimposed over the layout of West Side Grounds. The scope and timing of the construction makes it improbable that baseball could still played on the site after the ballpark was torn down in 1920. Note the Neuropsychiatric Institute at the southeast corner of the ballpark. (Illustration by author)

fans nutty or clueless enough to buy tickets for right field when Babe Ruth played.[12] There is little besides that letter available in the literature or elsewhere to support that statement, but the likely source lends it credence. Among several David Shulmans in the New York area—most too young to have seen Ruth play—one jumps through the screen. A lifelong word lover,

Cub aficionados Mike Reischl and Brian Bernardoni worked for years with the Illinois State Historical Society, the Illinois Medical District, and the University of Illinois at Chicago (UIC) to erect a marker commemorating the Chicago National League franchise's glory years on the West Side. The marker, written by Reischl, was unveiled in September 2008 in the 900 block of South Wood Street in Chicago. The spot is near West Side Grounds' center field clubhouse. Today, the UIC Neuropsychiatric Institute stands on the site, just down the street from the location, at the northwest corner of Wood and Polk streets, of the Cook County Detention Hospital for the "insane" and "feeble-minded" and its successor, the Cook County Psychopathic Hospital. Both fronted Polk Street and, thus, West Side Grounds' left field, supporting the claim that the idiom "out in left field" originated there. (Photograph by author)

this David Shulman was born November 12, 1912, which would mean his teenage years coincided with Ruth's years with the Yankees. He got his first library card in the Bronx, home to Yankee Stadium. In his 2004 obituary, the *New York Times* eulogized him as the "self-described Sherlock Holmes of Americanisms." He was more than a self-described idiom hunter; the *Times* noted in 1990 that "etymologist" Shulman had "contributed more than 5,000 words and phrases to the Oxford English Dictionary."[13] He also spent a great deal of time hunting down the true date of the Knickerbockers' first game under their set of baseball rules.[14] The love of language, the Bronx connection, and the dates all point to this David Shulman as the man who would pen a letter on the origin of an Americanism to William Safire's "On Language" column. This particular David Shulman likely would have taken these things too seriously to make up the "out in left field" story.[15]

Shulman's Yankee Stadium story also stands the test of baseball history. Indeed, one can wonder why anyone would buy left-field tickets over right-field seats during the Ruth era if he or she had a choice in the matter. Though he played across the outfield, the Bambino's preferred hunting ground was right field; in thirteen seasons at Yankee stadium, he averaged fifty games playing left field and seventy-seven playing right field. And then, there is batting. In his book *The Year Babe Ruth Hit 104 Home Runs*, Bill Jenkinson includes year-by-year "spray charts" of the left-handed batter's home runs.[16] An analysis of those charts reveals that, in home games at Yankee Stadium, Ruth averaged nineteen homers a year to right field, and less than one to left field. During the teenage years of David Shulman the etymologist—the 1926 through 1932 baseball seasons—Ruth averaged twenty-seven home runs to right field, and .83 to left field. He hit none there in '30, '31 or '32 . . . or '33 or '34 for that matter—all in time for the birth of "out in left field." If the Cubs pre-1916 theory is to be believed, then Yankees fans would have adopted the idiom after it originated in Chicago. Neither theory is a home run, but they're both likely in the ballpark, and are not necessarily mutually exclusive. Given the dates and the brick-and-mortar evidence in the West Side version, however, Chicago seems ahead in the count.

AGAIN, CHICAGO IS CHAMPION

FROM 1903 TO 1905, THE CUBS LIVED at or near the top of the league. The team finished second or third in each of those three years, Chance leading the team every time with batting averages above .300. Collectively, however, the team struggled at the plate with a combined .248 in 1904 and .245 in 1905. On the mound, a new star was emerging. There had been no one to claim the mantle of the great Clark Griffith, who won twenty-plus games for six straight seasons beginning in 1894 for the hapless Colts before being wooed to the White Sox by Charles Comiskey in 1901. Jack Taylor, until then a lackluster member of the staff, claimed the spotlight by posting back-to-back twenty-win seasons in 1902–1903. But he was traded to the Cardinals after being accused of acting to willingly lose three games against the Sox during the first City Series in 1903. That move set the stage for the three most glorious years in Cubs history. From St. Louis came Mordecai "Three Finger" Brown, a rookie with a 9-13 record. Brown's sinkerball, a natural pitch for him since he lost a finger as a child, helped him compile .600 seasons in 1904 and 1905. By the 1906 campaign, he was joined by left-hander Jack Pfiester to round up one of the most formidable pitching staffs in baseball.

Chance was now player-manager, elected to the position by the players after Frank Selee quit before the end of the 1905 season.[1] With the addition of Harry Steinfeldt at third and the resurgence of catcher Johnny Kling, a former .280-plus batter who had slumped the previous two years, the

Mordecai "Three Finger" Brown, whose pitching hand is seen here in 1911, was a major contributor to the Cubs' historic 1906–1910 run. He won 127 games over those five seasons, leading the staff every year but 1907. His 1906 ERA of 1.04 remains the lowest in Cubs history. Brown became one of the only Cubs World Series winners to play at what would become Wrigley Field, first in the Federal League in 1914–1915 and then again as a Cub in 1916. (Library of Congress LC-DIG-ppmsca-19495)

1906 lineup hit .260, tops in the league. Steinfeldt led the team in hitting (.327) and the league in runs (eighty-three). The team led the league in offense.[2] Behind the rubber, all six Cubs pitchers who appeared in more than fifteen games—including Taylor, who had returned once his alleged sin was forgiven or forgotten—compiled records better than .714, with a combined mark of 106-30. The staff's earned run average was 1.76. Add a win here or there by a couple of other Cubs pitchers, and the team finished the year with an all-time record 116 wins, twenty games ahead of the despised New York Giants.[3]

Across town, the White Sox enjoyed a banner year of their own, winning the American League with a 93-58 record. Because of their lowly .230 batting average, worst in the AL, Comiskey's players were known as the "Hitless Wonders." Their timid batting was offset by strong pitching. In addition to two twenty-game winners, their roster included Doc White, who had gone 18-6 (.750) with a 1.52 ERA. The stage was set for a conflagration between two of the most revered sports figures in the city, "Peerless Leader" Frank Chance and "Old Roman" Charles Comiskey, so nicknamed by the *Chicago Tribune*'s Charles Dryden.[4]

For a few weeks, baseball fever had gripped the city. In early September, with an all-Chicago World Series an almost foregone conclusion, the *Tribune* reported, "Chicago has gone stark, raving mad about baseball. The City has never witnessed a similar phenomenon, even in those dear dead days when the Chicago Colts, captain by the redoubtable A. C. Anson, were the most talked of baseball team in the world. The madness of Chicago of today is to those days as a raving cataract is to a placid mill pond.... The crowd the size of which was a record breaker last year is the ordinary crowd of this season."[5]

Since 1903, the champions of the National and American leagues met at the conclusion of their season in what was dubbed the World Series. The AL had humiliated the veteran league in the first contest, Boston beating Pittsburgh five games to three. The Series suffered a one-year hiatus because John Brush, owner of the Giants, refused to play AL champs Boston and what he judged an inferior league after winning the NL title. This led the leagues to formalize the concept of the World Series, rather than rely on loose agreements by the two league champs to play each other. New York did play in 1905 and reclaimed the mantle for the NL with a near-sweep of Philadelphia.[6] The baseball world was eager to see if the AL could rebound; one thing for sure was that a Chicago team would win it.

This was not the first time the two Chicago teams met. In 1903 and 1905, they had played in the postseason City Series, which locally provided major competition to the World Series. In '03, they had tied with seven victories each. Two years later, the Cubs had won it four games to one.[7]

Odds makers, ignoring that the Sox had put together a nineteen-game winning streak in September, had the Cubs as 2-to-1 favorites, with the figure as high as 3 to 1 in some quarters. Members of the Board of Trade bet $30,000. In the October 9 *Chicago Tribune*, Charles Dryden wrote a preview of the match-up: "Civil War breaks loose here today in Mr. Murphy's ball yard, and this morning sporting blood flows red and warm in the veins of the jungle. The big town on the rim of the lake is baseball dizzy, which is several degrees worse than batty."

Thirty-five years to the day after the city had been ablaze, the two Chicago teams made their way to the West Side Grounds for the opener of a seven-game, seven-day series. Snow flurries and cold, piercing rain greeted the brave souls who had decided to attend the game. The next day, Dryden would write, "Twelve thousand and odd pin wheels buzzing in their lids kept the brains of the chivalry and beauts from congealing." For those who could not or would not attend the games outdoors, the *Tribune* had prepared huge viewing parties at the First Regiment Armory and McVicker's Theater that could accommodate five thousand fans per game. At the theater, private wires fed the action to "baseball experts" who provided the play-by-play by megaphone, while the situation on the field was displayed on a twenty-square-foot scoreboard complete with an interactive diagram of the diamond. The Cubs had prepared with a grueling two-hour practice, while the Sox took in some vaudeville. Perhaps Chance, now the Cubs manager, should have listened to his own advice to save some hits for games by cutting good workouts short. The Sox beat the Cubs and "Three Finger" Brown 2–1 with the help of a triple by third baseman George Rohe, who had spent most of the season on the bench. The *Tribune*, which all year had referred to the West Siders as "Spuds" in honor of their new owner, Charles Murphy, who had bought the team from Spalding in 1905, summed up the game in two words: "Mashed Potatoes!" Dryden wrote what would become a double entendre more than one hundred years later: "The Cubs got the Rickets."[8]

Chance promised a victory in five games, and he looked like a fortune teller when the Cubs crushed their rivals at Sox Park the next day. Dryden summed it up in the October 11 *Tribune:* "Over in the stockyard district, where gentle deeds and smells are rare, the Cubs dragged the Sox around their own killing beds and slaughtered them to a finish. Score: 7 to 1. Surrounded by another 12,000 bunch of cold storage ladies and gentlemen and quite a lot of policemen, the losers of the first game showed the Sox how the national pastime should be exploited."[9] Thanks in part to Sox pitcher Ed Walsh's mastery of the spitball—the result of a mix of saliva, chewing gum, and tree sap—the Sox gained the edge with a 3–0 win on the West Side in game three. Someone let a hen in white stockings loose in the West Side Grounds outfield; though it was meant to mock the Sox, it failed to lay golden eggs for the Cubs. Dryden reported the Cubs had been "beaten by a nose," that of Sox outfielder Ed Hahn, who was hit by a pitch; "The blowing away of the nose filled the bases" and set-up Rohe's game-winning triple in the sixth inning. Everything seemed on the side of the White Sox—the hen spent much of the game near Hahn, whose name means "rooster" in German.[10] With better weather at Sox Park for game four, Brown held the South Siders to two hits for a 1–0 victory, Chance scoring the lone Cubs run on an Evers hit. The series was tied at two and neither team had yet won in its own ballpark.[11] The next day, West Side Grounds, renamed Pleurisy Park by Dryden as the weather turned cold again, could barely hold the record crowd—23,257. The *Tribune* described the scene: "The rest of the 30,000 rooters were outside the grounds, packed on adjoining roofs, clinging to telegraph poles and wire like monkeys." Inside, the Cubs wore gray out of superstition because they had not yet lost a game in that color. Board of Trade members bought some bear cubs that were paraded around the bases before the first pitch. The bears brought no more luck than the rooster. The Sox banged the Cubs around with twelve hits and won 8–6 in spite, the *Tribune* said, "of the rankest exhibition of fielding a team of champions ever gave in public"—the Hitless Wonders had come a long way, turning the tables on the Cubs, who only mustered six hits.[12]

Game Six was on the South Side, with nearly twenty thousand people inside the ballpark, and nearly as many outside. Upset at the long wait, meandering lines, and lack of available tickets, fans tore down the fence and got clubbed by more than fifty police officers, who could not keep as many as five hundred freeloaders from entering the stands alongside ticketholders. The contest was started early to avoid further mayhem. Finally, a team prevailed at home. West Side fans' hearts began to break as Mordecai Brown's fastballs refused to. Brown, pitching in his third game of the series, was clobbered and benched early, and the Cubs never recovered. In the first inning, as Brown unraveled, Frank Schulte fell while attempting a catch that would have retired the Sox and might have saved Brown. Chance screamed that his player had been tripped by a Sox fan. The umpire would not hear it and the onslaught continued. The Cubs lost 8–3 and the series 4-2. The Sox collected more than $1,900 each, while the Cubs took home $417.54, based on gate receipts and a special gift to his team by Charles Comiskey. More than two thousand Sox fans paraded through Chicago, going to as many homes of Sox players as they could find, chanting "What's de matter wid de White Sox? Dey're all right. Who's all right? De White Sox-x." The cartoon by McClutcheon on the front page of the *Tribune* said it all: Charles Comiskey was at home, his feet up, reading "Wild Bears I Have Met" surrounded by bear pelts. Publicly, Chance gave credit to the Sox for their surprise win, telling the *Tribune* the "greatest series ever played" had been "fairly" won. But in the locker room he deadpanned: "How that goddamn ball club ever beat us, I'll never understand."[13]

A few years later, reporter Hugh Fullerton offered an explanation that would pour salt in the wounds of Cubs fans, writing in a national publication: "Probably the most blindly loyal crowd in the world is that which follows the fortunes of the Chicago American league team, and to one who is disinterested the Chicago situation is acutely funny. The White Sox park is located on the South side of the city; the Cubs' on the west, and the city is divided into two great armed camps. In 1906 when these two teams, winners of the championships in their own leagues, met to contest for the Worlds' championship, it was the loyalty of the South Side crowd beyond doubt that won for the team."[14]

Crushing defeat aside, 1906 also meant the beginning of a Cubs tradition: being popular losers. Defeated by the Sox on the field, they edged them easily at the box office, outdrawing them by seventy thousand fans to break the 650,000 mark.[15]

Days after the Series, on October 20 and 21, the semipro Logan Squares— a group that played at Diversey and Milwaukee on the professional-ball-starved North Side and was not even the best in its Park Teams League— took on the White Sox and the Cubs. Playing with seven regulars, the Sox lost 2–1. Not even Mordecai Brown's pitching for the Cubs could save his team from a 1–0 loss.[16]

COVERING THE BASES

ONE THING CHICAGO POLITICIANS UNDERSTOOD all too well was the rare opportunity for posturing brought about by the first-ever crosstown World Series. On October 8, 1906, the first day of the series, the city council passed an ordinance proclaiming:

Whereas, the game of baseball has become known throughout the world as the national game of America, and

Whereas, Through the skill, ingenuity and sportsmanship of the management and members of the two base ball clubs representing the City of Chicago in the National League and American League, said clubs have brought to this city the pennants of their respective leagues for the championship of the season 1906; and

Whereas, The management of said baseball teams has therefore extended to this council the privilege of using their grounds for the purpose of playing benefit games of baseball; and

Whereas, This Council, representing the people of the City of Chicago, wishes to show its appreciation of true sportsmanship and the efforts of these two baseball clubs in further heralding the name of Chicago as the first city of the nation and a city to which success always comes; therefore be it

Resolved, That this Council extends its congratulations and best wishes to the management and the members of the baseball club representing the National League and of the baseball club representing the American League, and assures them of our hearty appreciation of their clean, wholesome support of the fair name of our city.[1]

Baseball and politics had long enjoyed close ties in Chicago. The White Stockings' season ticket ledger for 1878–1880 shows that complimentary books of tickets were distributed to the mayor, the city attorney, the city clerk, aldermen, the chief of police, and the commissioner of public works.[2] Many political heavyweights were Spalding's ownership partners in the 1880s and 90s. To buy the club in 1905, Charles Murphy received a loan of $100,000 from Charles Taft, brother of future U.S. president William Howard Taft.

World Series fever aside, local politicians were of great assistance in the day-to-day operation of the club. The Cubs were thus exempted of the requirement that teams not be located near churches, schools, or hospitals; a steeple towered over center field, and Cook County Hospital was located less than a block away.[3] Politics was useful to baseball, and baseball was useful in politics, at least locally and however short-lived the public's belief that high batting averages might equate with municipal efficiency. Spalding failed to ride his baseball fame to a California senatorial seat in the teens, but Anson, running as a Democrat, rode his baseball fame to his one term as city clerk in 1905 in a close election where Cap's batting average might have accounted for the 2,400 winning margin.[4]

The coziness with political figures did help develop a certain sense of entitlement in the mind of Spalding, who clearly thought his team deserved preferential treatment when he wrote to the superintendent of the streetcar company in 1885:

> Constant complaints are arising to me about the scarcity of cars. . . . It took [my brother] 50 minutes to go from my store to the grounds. The Van Buren St. line is the popular line to the grounds and for our mutual interest I would ask that you look into the matter and do what you can to help us out. We are draining at present an audience of about 2,000 to 2,500 people to each game and [for] the N.Y. games Sept. 29–31 Oct. 1 and 3 the attendance will probably average 8,000 to 10,000 people. Would it be possible to increase the number of cars to the grounds between the hours of 2:30 and 3:30?[5]

The club had enough pull to secure special favors from city hall. Although police were not usually assigned to protect private property, Chicago cops were diverted from other duties to keep order inside the park. They also directed traffic around the park and watched out for ticket scalpers. Spalding cut down on his expenditures thanks to the police posted at no cost within the grounds. He even secured Chicago cops for his store when World Series tickets went on sale.[6]

Although it was rumored that club officials, shady characters, and politicians were all in on a ticket-scalping scheme, something must have gone wrong in 1908, when Mayor Fred Busse threatened to close down the West Side Grounds, during the World Series no less, for building violations. The real reason, it turned out, was that the Cubs had failed to forward free tickets to his office.[7] That marked a stark contrast with 1906, when Alderman "Bathhouse" John Coughlin shut down city hall to allow his patronage workers to make it to the World Series.[8]

THREE MORE PENNANTS

IN THE FOUR YEARS AFTER THEIR DEFEAT to the Sox, the Cubs continued to assert themselves as one of the greatest dynasties in the history of the game. In 1907, while the reigning World Champions faltered on the South Side, the Cubs repeated as the best in the National League. Chance managed the team to a 107-45 finish, and led the club with a .293 batting average. Pittsburgh was a distant second, seventeen games behind, in spite of Honus Wagner's league-high .350. With the Chicago batsmen hitting .250 for the season—nobody hit above .300, and they ranked third in the league in batting—the pitchers surpassed themselves with a league-leading 1.73 staff ERA and thirty shutouts. Jack Pfiester's mark was 1.15. At the other end of the spectrum, Jack Taylor was dismissed after posting a 3.29 ERA, a performance that would probably earn millions in the majors today.[1] But could the staff muzzle Ty Cobb, the twenty-year-old batting champion who had powered Detroit to the AL pennant with a league-best .350 average?

The Tigers had compiled a 92-58 record, not all owing to offense. They had two twenty-five-game winners in Bill Donovan (25-4) and Ed Killian (25-13). But it was Cobb who had put them over the top. In his first full season as an everyday player, he had not just won the batting crown, he had obliterated the field. He came into the series having led the American League in slugging (.473), total bases (265), RBIs (119), and hits (212). His offensive threat didn't just come at the plate; he had stolen a league-best forty-nine bases over the course of the season. Not bad for a player making $2,400 a year.

At that price, he was a steal himself. Adjusted for inflation/deflation, Cobb's salary in 1907 was 33 percent higher than Anson's in 1876. He was making slightly less than Cubs ace Jack Pfiester, who had been signed in 1905 for $2,500, but more than Joe Tinker, who would make $1,500 a year until a modest raise in 1909. As player-manager, Frank Chance was in a class of his own; in 1906, management had given the Peerless Leader a chance to buy a 10-percent stake in the team, which he seized. Chance's salary was $5,500, plus his share of the profits. He would resell his ownership share by 1912.[2]

Back on the field, Cobb wasn't the only menace on the Tigers nine, either. Outfielder Sam Crawford had chalked up a .323 batting average, second only to Cobb in the AL, and added eighteen stolen bases.

Chance wasn't about to take chances. Murphy was adding temporary stands around the field to limit ground-rule doubles, which had plagued the Cubs in the '06 World Series, and to maximize gate receipts. Chance insisted right field be kept clear, to make life harder for lefties Cobb and Crawford. The scheme worked; Cobb left town hitting .167, owing in part to Chance's intuition and some memorable pitching by Cubs aces.[3]

The first game in Chicago, which drew nearly twenty-five thousand, was called on account of darkness with the score tied at three at the end of twelve innings. (The Cubs had tied the game in the bottom of the ninth as the Tigers' catcher let go of the third strike for what would have been the final out.) None of the following games were even close, and the Cubs gobbled up the Tigers in four games to win their first World Series. The Cubs helped their cause by stealing eighteen bases, and Steinfeldt hit .470. The team as a whole, however, batted just .257, its hitting more timely than mighty, and it was the pitchers who deserved the most credit for the sweep. Pfiester set the tone with a complete-game no-hitter in game two, and the rest of the staff held the Tigers to six, five, and seven hits over the next three games. The defense was also dominating, with catcher Johnny Kling denying seven of fourteen steal attempts by the Tigers. Over games two through five, Chicago outscored Detroit 16–3. Cobb was held to .200 for the series. This time, the Cubs pocketed $2,250 each, thanks more in part to a donation from owner Murphy than to gate receipts, which had been dismal in Detroit (seventy-three hundred fans attended game five). More than eight thousand people, the majority of whom had watched plays flash on a scoreboard over at the Tribune building on Dearborn, flooded several blocks in the Loop, blocking traffic. Streets had to be reopened by mounted police.[4]

Sy Sanborn put Chance on a pedestal in the October 13 *Tribune*: "Never before has a Chicago National league club won a world's championship, although this was the fourth world series in which a west side team has competed. It remained therefore for Frank L. (Fearless Leader) Chance to win for that big section of Chicago the trophy of supremacy and to write his name above that of A.C. Anson in the hearts of Chicago rooters, for Anson tried twice and failed."

The following season set the stage for one of the most breathtaking pennant races in Cubs history—as dramatic perhaps as that of 1969, and with a happier result. Chance and his men trailed the Giants at the end of August 1908, and a few weeks later were reduced to winning eleven of their last twelve to secure a tie. Such a run would be hard to stage for any team, but the Cubs' numbers foretold it might be near impossible for them. Evers's .300 average was the only mark above .276 among the regulars. Thankfully, though the pitching staff had slipped some, it maintained a 2.14 ERA.[5]

On September 23 came a game in New York that would alter the course of the pennant race and ruin reputations and lives because of what became known as "Merkle's boner." That day, at the end of the eighth, the Cubs and Giants were tied with one run apiece. The Cubs failed to score in the ninth. At the bottom of the inning, with a man on base and two outs, nineteen-year-old Fred Merkle advanced the runner to third with a single. A single to center by the next Giants hitter brought about the winning run and an exuberant celebration by New York fans, who spilled onto the field. Merkle, perhaps caught up in the celebration or perhaps running for safety from the fans, headed straight for the dugout without ever touching second. But Evers screamed for the ball. What happened next could never be sorted out, and there are many versions, but there is no question that a ball appeared in Evers's hand. Just days earlier, umpire Hank O'Day had let such a run stand in a Cubs game against Pittsburgh, and Evers would recall in his 1910 book *Touching Second* (was he rubbing it in?) that O'Day had turned away to take a drink and had not seen the runner miss the base. But this time O'Day called the out, which nullified the run and the game, which the crowd precluded from resuming. Because of the tie, the game would be replayed in New York at the end of the regular season. Evers referred to O'Day's call and refusal to reverse it in face of the mob of fans as "one of the greatest examples of individual heroism the game has known."[6]

In the evening edition of the September 23 *Tribune* after the game, Charles Dryden reported the comical chain of events after Merkle trotted off the field without touching the base, chased by his captain at the same time that his third-base coach McGinnity rushed on the field to head off a protest by the screaming Cubs. It is well worth a read through its conclusion:

> Hoffman fielded Brickwell's knock and threw to Evers for a force play on the absent Merkle. But McGinnity, who was not in the game, cut in ahead and grabbed the ball before it reached the eager Trojan. Three Cubs from as many directions landed on the iron man at the same time and jolted the ball from his cruel grasp. It rolled among the spectators who had swarmed upon the diamond like an army of starving potato bugs.
>
> At this thrilling juncture "Kid" Kroh, the demon southpaw, swarmed upon the human potato bugs and knocked six of them galley-west. The triumphant Kroh passed the ball to Steinfeldt after cleaning up the gang that had it. Tinker wedged in and the ball conveyed to Evers for the force out of Merkle, while Capt. Donlin was still some distance off towing that brilliant young gent by the neck.
>
> Some say Merkle eventually touched second base, but not until he had been forced out by Hoffman to McGinnity, to six potato bugs, to Kroh, to some more Cubs, and the shrieking, triumphant Mr. Evers, the well-known Troy shoe dealer. There have been some complicated plays in baseball, but we do not recall one just like this in a career of years of monkeying with the national pastime.

In a 1914 *Tribune* story written by Sanborn, O'Day, by then the Cubs' manager and speaking about the incident on the record for the first time, would claim that the role played by Evers—whom he succeeded as skipper—had been overblown:

> Evers was made famous by that Merkle play in 1908 and was not in on it at all. . . . We did not make the decision at New York because Evers is supposed to have touched second base when Merkle started for the clubhouse, but because Joe McGinnity, when the ball was thrown back to

the infield by Artie Hofman, interfered with one of the Cub players who got the ball. I think it was Joe Tinker. Evers stood at second base and did not know what was coming off until Tinker ran over and grabbed [umpire] Emslie to call his attention to the fact that Merkle had not touched second base.

The same article quoted Tinker—himself not without a checkered history with Evers—with a slightly different take that corroborated Evers's lack of involvement but also captured the total mayhem that day in a way that, if true, would reflect even worse on the umpires for losing control of the situation and having no earthly clue what was taking place, and thus might explain why O'Day might opt for a different spin:

It was Pfiester with whom McGinnity wrestled. Jack picked up the ball after Hofman's throw hit me in the back of the neck. I was running over to inform Emslie that Merkle had not touched second. McGinnity got the ball away from Pfelster and threw it in the back of third base. The crowd was out on the field by that time and a spectator got the ball. Harry Steinfedlt ran over and fought for the ball, but did not get it until Pitcher Krohran over and punched the man who had it. Steinfeldt then ran over to second base, and, instead of touching second himself, handed the ball to Evers, who stood there while all the wrangling was taking place.[7]

Given the reigning confusion that September 23, and the multiple and diverging agendas of those involved, no one will ever know exactly what happened, except that the Cubs came out on top.

On October 4, 1908, a record crowd of 30,247 assembled at West Side Grounds for the crucial last regular-schedule game before the Cubs' make-up match-up against the Giants. The 97-55 Cubs needed a win over 98-55 Pittsburgh to retain a shot at the pennant. In Pittsburgh, fifty thousand were assembled downtown to hear the game reported via megaphone from newspaper offices. Five thousands New Yorkers gathered at the Polo Grounds to take in the play-by-play via a scoreboard. Mordecai Brown helped his own cause by bringing in Tinker's winning run with a single in front of the now-record crowd of 30,248, as a woman had just given birth in the stands. She refused to give her name and there were no reports of her being admitted at any West Side hospital after receiving medical care in the

Cubs' clubhouse. The identity of the "baseball baby" remains a mystery. Meanwhile, the 95-55 Giants needed to win their next three games before their final game against the Cubs.[8]

By October 8, New York had done just that to tie Chicago for first. The two teams were facing each other for the pennant at the Polo Grounds in front of thirty-five thousand. The atmosphere bordered on hysterical, as New York fans physically assaulted several players including Chance, who ended up with broken cartilage in his neck, while Pfiester was stabbed and hit in the shoulder.

Brown, who had been the victim of O'Day's call in the Pittsburgh game, out-pitched the Giants' Christy Mathewson, who had been the victim of O'Day's September 23 call. It was Brown's twenty-ninth win of the season. Tinker sealed the deal at the plate. The Cubs earned their third straight World Series appearance with a 4–2 victory and had to be escorted off the field and out of the city by police with guns drawn.

There were even more dire consequences from the Merkle incident. Merkle, who went on to have a successful sixteen-year career (part of it with the Cubs in the late 1910s) could never shake off the "Bonehead" nickname. National League President Harry Pulliam, who already thought the owners had been conspiring against him, went into a deep depression after facing public scorn when he ruled against an appeal by the Giants. He killed himself in July 1909.[9]

After such a lead-in, the World Series could only be anticlimactic. The Tigers, too, had repeated, winning the AL by a half game over Cleveland and 1½ games over the White Sox.

Again, Cobb had won the batting crown and dominated most offensive categories. The Tigers' line-up was nearly identical to 1907, and the Cubs had exactly the same one. Really, all that had changed going into the series was that Cobb had doubled his salary to $4,800. And that's all that would change.

The Cubs again tamed the Tigers, again stealing bases at will, and won it four games to one. In game one, though, it had looked like it was going to be a whole different year for Detroit, until the Cubs scored five runs in the ninth to win the opener 10–6.

Ed Reulbach had gone 24-7 on the season and had recorded two complete-game shutouts in the same day on September 26 against Brooklyn; he led a

Fans in front of the Cubs Clubhouse at a World Series game in 1908. (Chicago History Museum S054691)

staff that only faltered once (Pfeister lost game three, 8–3). Chance hit .421 for the series, Schulte .389, and Evers .350. Cobb did rebound with a .368 average, but as a team the Tigers had been muzzled again. They were even blanked in the last two games. The Cubs became the first team ever to win two straight titles.[10] The domination was so complete that attendance was the lowest in years for the World Series and that the October 15 *Daily News* decreed the completed bouts a "quiet, dry affair."

The series would be remembered for one play in the final game. In the fourth inning, the October 15 *Daily News* reported, Cobb came to bat with men on first and second. "Make him bunt," Chance ordered pitcher Mordecai Brown, "so that you, Brown, can get the ball; Steinfeldt will stay glued to third, his foot on the bag, and when you get the chance shoot it to Steinfeldt and force O'Leary." As so many other times before, the Cubs were the gifted puppets of mastermind Chance. The trick was to get a bunt that would be playable to third, and Brown and the *Daily News'* writer delivered:

> Ty saw his chance, bunted it and sped to first. The ball rolled to that one immune spot, along the line.
>
> Brownie had planned it. He had the jump. He was in motion with the bat. It was the foreknowledge that gave him the mastery of the situation. He was after the ball before it was tapped. Mind and body worked together with the speed and grace of a cat after a mouse. Facing the foul line, "Brownie" grabbed that ball and, turning the shortest way, to the right, thus having to make only a half turn to see third, he shot that ball with unerring accuracy into Steinfeldt's hands.

The Tigers would never come back, and the paper declared them "outclassed."[11]

Although they won 104 games in 1909, five more than the previous year, the Cubs could not overcome the Pirates, who claimed the pennant with 110 victories and continued the NL's domination over Detroit by beating Cobb and the Tigers 4-3 in the series.[12] Many must have wondered how the season would have turned out had catcher Johnny Kling not sat out 1909 over a salary dispute.[13] In the three prior pennant-winning seasons, Kling had batted .312, .284, and .276 and averaged above .980 in fielding. His replacements for 1909 were subpar. Former Tiger Jimmy Archer could only muster .230 and .960 over eighty games and Pat Moran .220 and .984 over seventy-seven games. As the team struggled somewhat without him, Kling managed semipro ball and even won the world pocket billiards championship.[14]

Thanks to a Pittsburgh collapse in 1910, the Cubs' repeat of 104 victories was this time good enough to earn a fourth World Series appearance in five years. Kling was back with the team, with a new $4,500 salary. The Giants were a distant second, thirteen-games behind.

But the Cubs did not have the Tigers to kick around anymore; the team would play the surging Philadelphia Athletics instead. Sidelined by a broken leg, Evers was missing from the lineup. His replacement, Heinie Zimmerman, was no equal to the smart, agile Evers. The infield's chemistry was affected, but what happened at the plate proved decisive. The once invincible pitching staff was knocked around for fifty-six hits in five games, and the Athletics won 4-1. Chicago was outscored 35–15. Two Philadelphia

This October 15, front page 1908 cartoon in the *Chicago Daily News* shows the Cubs cleaning house. (Author's collection)

players hit above .400 for the series, and pitcher Jack Coombs recorded three wins. Among the Cubs starters, Chance and Schulte led the way with .353, and Tinker was not far behind with .333. But Zimmerman struggled with .235, while Steinfeldt and Kling, the new big-money man, stunk with .100 and .077, respectively.

The 1908 pennant, stamped with a bear, can be seen flying over center field (along with rooftops on nearby buildings) in this shot of the 1909 City Series at West Side Grounds. (Library of Congress LC-DIG-ds-04594, restoration by author)

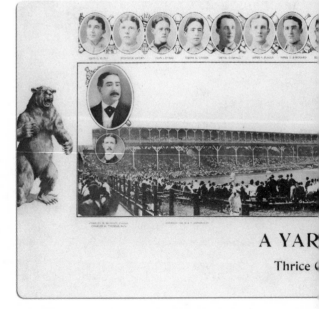

A 1908 poster commemorated one of the greatest runs in baseball history. (Chicago History Museum Ichi-03974)

X vs CUBS
NSHIP SERIES
West Side Park.

COPYRIGHT 1908 by
THE GEO. R. LAWRENCE Co
CHICAGO NEW YORK
5-2867 B

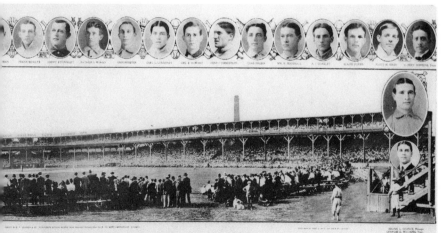

F THE NATIONAL GAME

HOME OF THE RECORD-BREAKING CUBS

ns of The National League 1906-1907-1908
Champions of The World-1908

The *Daily News* cut to the chase drily in its lead: "Philadelphia Athletics, aggressive, spirited and buoyant with the enthusiasm of youth yesterday out-batted, out-fielded and outpitched the veteran Chicago Cubs."[15] Yet in the loss, the Cubs each made as much off the gate receipts—$1,300—as in their 1908 win, thanks to higher attendance in Philadelphia than Detroit, though Murphy did not pitch in with a bonus.[16] The Cubs dynasty had taken its last breath. From 1906 through 1910, Chance and his men had compiled a winning percentage of .693, which to this day remains the best five-year run of any team in baseball history.[17] The streak would also make owners Charles Murphy and Charles Taft rich men. They had paid Spalding $105,000 for the team in 1905, and had proceeded to make $165,000 in 1906 alone. Over 1907–1913, they made $810,000, or $19 million in 2013 dollars. That represented an 800-percent return, and made the collective $7,000 bonus to the 1907 team seem like crumbs.[18]

GOING, GOING . . .

CHANCE ESSENTIALLY TOOK HIMSELF OUT of the lineup in 1911, when he batted .239 over thirty-one games.[1] Evers batted .226 in just forty-six games, the victim of a nervous breakdown likely owing to the bankruptcy of a side business and a car accident in which he was the driver and his best friend was killed.[2] Catcher Johnny Kling was traded. On the mound, King Cole (18-7) and "Three Finger" Brown (21-11) anchored a squad that still got the wins but whose earned-run average was "slipping" to reach almost 3.00. Two players prevented the team from sliding farther than second place and 7½ games behind. The first standout of 1911 was Wildfire Schulte who, in his eighth season on the West Side, batted above .300 for the second straight year—the only two times he hit that mark. The other, newcomer Heinie Zimmerman, took over Evers's spot and hit .307, an encouraging start that would be confirmed in 1912 when he hit .372, best in the National League, with 207 runs and 103 runs batted in. Evers's spectacular .347-hitting returned that year, which, paired with Zimmerman's league-leading performance, could not offset cracks throughout the Cubs organization. The team fell to third place. Late in the season, Chance was fired by Murphy. The official reason for the dismissal was a 16-0 loss to the White Sox in the City Series, but trouble had been brewing for months.[3] Channeling Spalding and Anson, Murphy claimed the team's regular-season woes owed to drunkenness and carousing, while Chance felt Murphy was not putting up the money needed to field a winning squad and was blaming the team for some "hard luck." Murphy insisted on barring the players from drinking, smoking, and being out past midnight, over Chance's objection. At issue was really who was boss of the team.[4] The tension between the men was not new, and Chance recalled that after the championship years, "I had to threaten to quit in order to get my salary lifted to $10,000. Murphy would argue that I had some stock in the club and ought to be satisfied with that. Well, I bought that stock and I worked hard for it."[5]

Chance had seen the end of his tenure coming. In October 1912, the *Chicago Tribune* asked him to pen a series of articles about the upcoming Cubs-Sox City Series. He wrote that he would be covering "what may be my last series of games as manager of the Chicago Cubs. . . . It's up to Mr. Murphy. I have not resigned."[6]

After the 1912 season, in a move that seemed as natural as it proved catastrophic, Evers was elected manager, with Murphy's blessing. The announcement coincided with the declaration that Murphy would build a new concrete-and-steel ballpark over the site of the West Side Grounds' left field and adjacent vacant land along Polk Street. History would dictate otherwise. Tinker, who also had applied for the job and for whom dealing with Evers's foul mood on the field was one thing but dealing with him as a boss was quite another, demanded to be traded over the winter. Jimmy Sheckard, one of the mainstays on the team since 1906, also left the team.

Throughout 1913, arguments and near fistfights between players and Evers were not rare. Probably because of the dugout's atmosphere, Zimmerman got ejected three times in five days in June. At season's end, Chicago was third, 13½ games behind New York. Even though the *Tribune* credited the team with playing the best baseball in the league after August 1, the handwriting was on the wall when in the fall, President Murphy let it be known that "Evers is a great ball player, but too impulsive to be a manager and a player at the same time." Evers was shipped to Boston, just one year into a five-year contract, marking the end of an era.[7]

In 1914, perhaps in an attempt to recapture their old luck, the Cubs named former "Bonehead" play umpire Hank O'Day their manager. But the stars slumped, and several unknowns made names for themselves only in terms of futility. The ensuing fourth-place finish earned O'Day the pink slip.[8]

As if the Cubs' faltering fortunes that year were not enough to hurt attendance, the team found itself competing for fans not only with the White Sox but also an entry from the upstart Federal League. Again, Chicago was a key player in the inception of a new league. Local businessman John Powers had decided in 1913 to follow in the footsteps of Hulbert and Comiskey. He started the Columbian League, a Midwest circuit, which quickly faltered. But the next year, 1914, he and five others set up the Federal League on much stronger footing. With teams in Chicago, Indianapolis, Cleveland, Kansas City, Pittsburgh, and St. Louis, the new outfit was going head-to-head with the two major leagues. The league shrewdly recruited wealthy sponsors in each city. Charles Weeghman, owner of ten Loop restaurants, and William Walker, a wholesale fish distributor, bought the Chicago Feds in mid-1913 and built Weeghman Park on Chicago's North Side, a part of town long ignored by the major leagues. The field, located at Addison and Clark streets, gave a permanent home to the Feds, who had previously played at DePaul University. While paying lip service to the reserve clause, the Federals recruited heavily from major-league ranks. In December 1913, Weeghman introduced Joe Tinker as his player-manager. When $250,000 Weeghman Park opened on April 23, 1914, the Federal League had grown to include entries from Brooklyn and Baltimore. The new stadium was modeled after New York's Polo Grounds and could seat fourteen thousand. Despite the Feds being in the thick of the pennant race until the last week of the season, attendance lagged—the squad was, after all, mostly made up of minor leaguers.

After watching his team finish second to Indianapolis and borrowing funds from his restaurant business, Weeghman signed Mordecai "Three Finger" Brown and Walter Johnson to anchor his pitching staff. But Charles Comiskey paid Johnson to stay out of Chicago and, realizing that they would not be granted major-league status, Federal owners sued the NL and AL in Chicago in January 1915. They attacked the reserve clause and the management of the leagues for violating the Anti-Trust Act. Judge Kenesaw Mountain Landis hinted he would side with the majors, but added he would reserve his judgment for a year. This was enough to push both sides to the negotiating table.

When the negotiations ground to a halt, Weeghman tried gimmick after gimmick to draw fans for the 1915 season, from renaming his team the Chicago Whales to enlisting Mayor "Big Bill" Thompson to appear at the park. In the process, Weeghman held Mordecai Brown Day and Joe Tinker Day to lure away Cubs fans. Still, attendance was lackluster.

This bear cub walking off the field at West Side Grounds in 1906 would be followed by the real-life Cubs in 1916, who would migrate north to what would become known as Wrigley Field. (Chicago History Museum S052235)

Meanwhile, on the West Side, the Cubs were not faring much better. Finishing in fourth place with a .477 record, they were largely ignored, having posted their first sub-.500 season since 1902. At what was not only the last home game of the season but, it would turn out, the last ever regular-season contest at West Side Grounds, "not more than 3,000 were present [...] and most of them were inquiring what the Whales were doing on the North Side. No scores were posted, however, on the 'outlaw' combat."[9]

When the Whales won the pennant by .000854, the major leagues refused to include them in the World Series. The Cubs and Sox also turned down their request for participation in the City Series. The latter probably hurt the Whales' bottom line more so than the former. The previously episodic series had been played every year since 1911 (the Sox winning each time) and had become the premier sporting event in the city. But, in 1915, it was not a big money maker, at least for the players. They were to share only in the purse of the first four games—out of fourteen contests—which were played during the week. One bitterly cold day, on which a regular-season game might have been cancelled, the contest was played, prompting one White Sox player to deadpan "leave it to the big bosses to cap all the dough." All told, the Cubs received $295 each as the losing team (3-11 for the series) and the Sox $423. "At least," the *Tribune* commented, "each man will get enough to buy coal for the winter."[10] Meanwhile, owners were holding talks over record amounts of money. Mounting financial trouble at the Federal League level forced a new round of talks with the majors and, in December 1915, the Whales were absorbed.

GONE

ONE FEDERAL OWNER WAS ALLOWED TO BUY the St. Louis Browns while Weeghman gained control of the Cubs from Charles Taft for $500,000 in January 1916. Among his financial partners were J. Ogden Armour, of meatpacking fame, and William Wrigley Jr., of the chewing gum empire. The Baltimore team, left out of the agreement, sued the major leagues; the U.S. Supreme Court closed the book on the *Federal Baseball Club v. National League* case in 1922 with its famous ruling that baseball was a form of entertainment not subject to the Sherman Antitrust Act. Weeghman began his tenure as Cubs president by merging the Whales' and Cubs' rosters and moving the team to the newer North Side stadium, which would now sometimes be called Cubs Park, a name that by the end of the decade would be the sole one in use.[1]

On April 16, 1916—four days ahead of the Cubs' first game ever at Clark and Addison—Ring Lardner's "In the Wake of the News" column in the *Chicago Tribune* was a eulogy of the old ballpark on the West Side:

> Now fades the glimmering landscape on the sight.
> Save for the chatter of the laboring folk,
> Returning to their hovels for the night,
> All is still at Taylor, Lincoln, Wood and Polk.
> Beneath this aged roof, this grandstand's shade,

Where peanuts shucks lie in a mold'ring heap,
Where show the stains of pop and lemonade,
The Cub bugs used to cheer and groan and weep.

Nearly bankrupt, Weeghman borrowed heavily from Wrigley, who assumed ownership in 1918.[2] That year, the North Side Cubs won the pennant, but lost the World Series 4-2 to the Boston Red Sox. In 1919, Charles Murphy sold West Side Grounds to the State of Illinois for $400,000, the equivalent of $5 million in 2013. "This sale of the old west side park to the state definitely settles the rumor that the Cubs planned moving back to the west side, where baseball always has drawn heavier crows than it does on the north side," the *Tribune* said.[3]

In August 1920, Weeghman's restaurants were thrown into receivership.[4] Had Frank Chance and Charles Murphy had their way, Cubs fans may never have set foot in "Wrigley." The two moved past their differences to try to buy the team from Wrigley, but they were rebuffed.[5] On August 5, the *Chicago Tribune* reported:

> There is little that appeals to sentiment in the announcement there is for sale a mass of lumber on the west side in the city of Chicago. Some one million square feet are thrown on the market, and with the sale of this lumber the saws of a wrecking company buzz a requiem and awaken memories of hundreds of thousands of baseball fans.
>
> It is the end of the Chicago National League baseball park that was—Polk, Lincoln and Wood Streets.
>
> This famed landmark of baseball, the home of world champions and league champions, where heroes of the diamond cavorted in battles for baseball supremacy on the green before admiring thousands, is doomed. The wrecking company is attending to that.

On Opening Day 1927, the new ballpark was officially called Wrigley Field.[6] By that time, the site of West Side Grounds was mostly occupied by the newly constructed medical campus of the University of Illinois. Today, amid the Gothic Revival buildings, there is a grass courtyard. Located over the old right-center field, just off Johnny Evers's second base, this Chicago field of dreams is too small for a ball game, but big enough to play catch with the past.

Comprising part of West Side Grounds' old infield—where Tinker, Evers, and Chance plied their trade and the Cubs won their last World Series—this courtyard at the University of Illinois of Chicago makes a literal Field of Dreams for Cub fans. (Photograph by author)

ABOUT THE BALLPARKS:
STADIUMS OF THE CHICAGO CUBS
AND THEIR ANCESTORS

1870   Dexter Park—Corner of 42nd and Halsted streets

1871   Lake Park—Bounded by Michigan Avenue, Randolph Street, Madison Street, and Lake Michigan

1874–1877   23rd Street Grounds—Bounded by 22nd, 23rd, State, and Clark streets

1878–1884   Lakefront Park—Same location as Lake Park

1885–1890   West Side Park—Bounded by Congress, Throop, Loomis, and Harrison streets

1891   West Side Park (half of games)

       Brotherhood Park, aka South Side Grounds (half of games)— Northwest corner of 35th Street and Wentworth Avenue

1892   Brotherhood Park

1893   Brotherhood Park (most games)

       West Side Grounds (Sundays only)—Polk, Wood, Taylor, and Lincoln (Wolcott) streets

1894–1915   West Side Grounds

1916–?   Weeghman Park, aka Cubs Park, aka Wrigley Field—Bounded by Clark and Addison streets and Sheffield and Waveland avenues

THE TEAM THROUGH
THE DECADES

1870s

Record: 250-194, 1 pennant

Following years of amateur and semipro baseball in Chicago, the Chicago White Stockings are among the charter members of the National Association of Professional Base Ball Players (NAPBBP), created in 1871. The team goes on hiatus in 1872–1873 after the Chicago Fire, which destroys the team's ballpark on the southeast corner of Randolph and Michigan. Some former White Stockings form a semipro team, but Chicago is not represented in the NAPBBP until the return of the White Stockings, now also called the Chicagos, in 1874. In 1876, the National League is created, at the initiative of Chicagoan William Hulbert. Having recruited key players from Boston's championship team of 1872–1875, along with Adrian Anson, the White Stockings win the inaugural league pennant under skipper Al Spalding. Anson becomes manager in 1879.

Results (number of teams in parentheses if other than 8):
1870: 1st—*contested*
1871: 3rd
1874: 5th
1875: 6th (13 teams)
1876: 1st
1877: 5th (6)
1878: 4th (6)
1879: 4th

1880S

Record: 691-395, 5 pennants

With "Cap" Anson at the helm, the White Stockings/Chicagos have the best decade in franchise history, with five first-place finishes in the National League, along with five league batting titles, four no-hitters, and a total of sixteen twenty-game-winning seasons by six different pitchers. Their domination is not supreme, as they lose the newly organized Championship of the World to the American Association's St. Louis Browns in 1885 and 1886.

Results:
1880: 1st
1881: 1st
1882: 1st
1883: 2nd
1884: 4th
1885: 1st
1886: 1st
1887: 3rd
1888: 2nd
1889: 3rd

1890S

Record: 710-654, no pennant

After a mass defection to the Players' League in 1890, the White Stockings become known as the Colts. Anson oversees several years of futility after 1891, which eventually costs him his job after the 1897 season, though his successor fails to do much better. With Anson gone, the press christens the team the Orphans.

Results:
1890: 2nd
1891: 2nd
1892: 7th (12 teams)
1893: 9th (12)
1894: 8th (12)
1895: 4th (12)
1896: 5th (12)
1897: 9th (12)
1898: 5th
1899: 6th

1900S

Record: 879-592, 3 pennants, 2 World Series titles

Another mass exodus of players in 1901, this time to the newly formed American League, earns the team the name of Remnants. Across town, the AL repurposes the dormant White Stockings name. The year 1902 marks a turning point, with new manager Frank Selee undertaking the team's rebuilding. Lackluster catcher Frank Chance is turned into a first baseman; Johnny Evers and Joe Tinker are brought on in 1902, and Mordecai "Three Finger" Brown follows in 1904. Brown and Chance, who becomes player-manager in 1905, dominate the next several years. Chance leads the team in every major offensive category for the decade, except home runs. Brown accumulates 135 wins and an ERA of 1.51. The new blood brings about a new name for the squad, the Cubs, which slowly takes hold beginning in 1902, though it competes with Spuds in 1906 owing to the arrival of a new Irish team owner, Charles Murphy. The team goes on to post the best five-year winning percentage of any team in baseball history—topped with World Series wins in 1907 and 1908 against Ty Cobb's Detroit Tigers, combined with a bitter Series loss in 1906 against the crosstown White Sox.

Results:
1900: 5th
1901: 6th
1902: 5th
1903: 3rd
1904: 2nd
1905: 3rd
1906: 1st
1907: 1st
1908: 1st
1909: 2nd

1910S

Record (through 1915): 526-392, 1 pennant

The decade starts well enough, with a return to the World Series in 1910, though the Cubs lose to the Philadelphia Athletics. The wheels slowly fall off after that. Evers misses most of 1911 because of a nervous breakdown. Chance stops playing early in 1912 for health reasons, and is fired as manager at the end of the year. Evers takes over, but Tinker quits as a result. The Cubs still average ninety-plus wins in 1911–1913, but the last few years have placed the bar and the expectations of fans and management very high. The team further falters through the distraction of the Federal League in 1914–1915, whose pennant-winning franchise plays at Clark and Addison on the North Side with men named Brown and Tinker. Though the Federal League folds, its Chicago team, the Whales, merges with the Cubs, who move north to what will become Wrigley Field.

Results:
1910: 1st
1911: 2nd
1912: 3rd
1913: 3rd
1914: 4th
1915: 4th

NOTES

INTRODUCTION

1. Though ivy has come to be synonymous with Wrigley Field, the ivy on the stadium's outfield wall was in fact not planted until 1937. See Glenn Stout, *The Cubs*, 153.

CHAPTER 1. FROM LITTLE ENGLISH ACORN
TO GIANT AMERICAN OAK

1. Albert Spalding, *America's National Game: Historic Facts Concerning the Beginning, Evolution, Development, and Popularity of Base Ball* (New York: American Sports Publishing, 1911), 263.

2. Ibid., 4.

3. Warren Goldstein, *Playing for Keeps: A History of Early Baseball* (Ithaca, N.Y.: Cornell University Press, 1989), 21.

4. Spalding, *America's National Game*, 19.

5. Ibid.

6. Peter Levine, *A.G. Spalding and the Rise of Baseball: The Promise of American Sport* (New York: Oxford University Press, 1986), 113.

7. David Quentin Voigt, *Baseball: An Illustrated History* (University Park: Penn State University Press, 1987), 5; Spalding, *America's National Game*, 7, 20–21, 47.

8. Daniel Okrent and Peter Levine, *The Ultimate Baseball Book* (Boston: Houghton Mifflin, 1984), 12. In 1947, Rickey brought Jackie Robinson into the major leagues.

9. Henry Chadwick, *The Game of Baseball: How to Learn It, How to Play It, and How to Teach It* (New York: George Munro, 1868), 9–10.

10. William Ryczek, *Baseball's First Inning: A History of the National Pastime Through the Civil War* (Jefferson, N.C.: McFarland, 2009), 39.

11. Benjamin Rader, *Baseball: A History of America's Game* (Champaign: University of Illinois Press, 2008), 9.

12. Spalding does not deny the existence of Town Ball and Massachusetts Ball but assigns them post-Doubleday birth dates (p. 39).

13. Cited in Voigt, *Baseball: An Illustrated History*, 7.

14. Cited in Goldstein, *Playing for Keeps*, 158, note 11.

15. Ryczek, *Baseball's First Inning*, 39. For an in-depth discussion of the game's origins, see Ryczek's book as well as Dean Sullivan's *Early Innings: A Documentary History of Baseball, 1825–1908* (Lincoln: University of Nebraska Press, 1995)

16. Gare Thompson, *The Southeast: Its History and its People* (Independence, Ky.: National Geographic School Publishing, 2003), 11.

17. Voigt, *Baseball: An Illustrated History*, 8–9; Marty Appel, *The First Book of Baseball* (New York: Crown Publishers, 1990), 6, 39; Spalding, *America's National Game,* 65–70; Rader, *Baseball: A History,* 15; Ryczek, *Baseball's First Inning,* 33–35. Though the widely accepted date for the first account of the first Knickerbocker game is October 21, 1845, etymologist David Shulman found a possible October 6, 1845 game, which he dubbed the possible "phantom first game of baseball." See "About New York; On Baseball, Too, A Maven Seeks the Last Word," *New York Times,* October 17, 1990.

CHAPTER 2. THE BASEBALL FRONTIER

1. Federal Writers' Project (Illinois), Works Progress Administration, *Baseball in Old Chicago* (Chicago: A.C. McClurg, 1939), 1; Alfred Spink, *The National Game: A History of Baseball* (St. Louis: National Game Publishing, 1910), 63: Spink reports a game played in the city in 1856 but does not provide a source, and gives as the first published report of organized baseball in the city a May 1, 1859 article in *The Spirit of the Times* of New York.

2. Mark Rucker and John Freyer, *19th Century Baseball in Chicago* (Charleston, S.C.: Arcadia Publishing, 2003), 16.

3. Ibid., 23.

4. Goldstein, *Playing for Keeps,* 30–31, 34–35.

5. Federal Writers' Project, *Baseball in Old Chicago,* 3.

6. George Kirsch, *Baseball in Blue and Gray: The National Pastime During the Civil War* (Princeton, N.J.: Princeton University Press, 2003), 31–32.

7. Voigt, *Baseball: An Illustrated History,* 10–12; Stephen Freedman, "The Baseball Fad in Chicago, 1865–1870: An Exploration of the Role of Sport in the Nineteenth-Century City," Journal of Sport History (Summer 1978): 42–43.

8. Kirsch, *Baseball in Blue and Gray,* 117.

9. Goldstein, *Playing for Keeps,* 73.

10. Federal Writers' Project, *Baseball in Old Chicago,* 3.

11. Ibid., 3; Larry Names, *Bury My Heart at Wrigley Field: The History of the Chicago Cubs* (Neshkoro, Wisc.: Sportsbook Publishing, 1990), 31–34.

12. Freedman, "Baseball Fad in Chicago," 42.

13. Voigt, *Baseball: An Illustrated History,* 9, 12.

14. Freedman, "Baseball Fad in Chicago," 43–45.

15. Ibid., 54–56.

16. Spink, *National Game,* 64.

17. *Chicago Daily Tribune,* July 2, 1870.

18. Chadwick, *Game of Baseball,* 10.

19. Ibid., 94–107.

20. Voigt, *Baseball: An Illustrated History,* 13.

21. Spalding, *America's National Game,* 119–22.

22. Chadwick, *Game of Baseball,* 142.

23. Federal Writers' Project, *Baseball in Old Chicago,* 23.

24. Ibid., 11.

25. Ibid., 25.

26. Hulbert Family Papers, manuscript, Chicago History Museum. Letter to Ethelyn Hulbert, July 2, 1875

27. *Chicago Tribune,* July 2, 1875.

CHAPTER 3. CHICAGO'S HIRED GUNS

1. Federal Writers' Project, *Baseball in Old Chicago,* 4–5. In June 1866, the Excelsiors competed against their hometown rivals, the Atlantics, and teams from Milwaukee, Detroit, Bloomington, Rockford, and Freeport. The following year they prevailed against nines from St. Louis, Peoria, Ottawa, Louisville, Milwaukee, Freeport, Quincy, Freeport, and Jacksonville, Illinois, and the Chicago Pacifics.

2. Spink, *National Game,* 63.

3. Spalding, *America's National Game,* 123; Voigt, *Baseball: An Illustrated History,* 24, 27.

4. Spalding, *America's National Game,* 138–39.

5. Spink, *National Game,* 9.

6. Voigt, *Baseball: An Illustrated History,* 33.

7. William Ryczek, *When Johnny Came Sliding Home: The Post-Civil War Baseball Boom, 1865–1870* (Jefferson, N.C.: McFarland, 2006), 202–5; Names, *Bury My Heart,* 30.

8. Federal Writers' Project, *Baseball in Old Chicago,* 7.

9. Art Ahrens, "How the Cubs Got Their Name," *Chicago History* (Spring 1976): 39; Spink, *National Game*, 65, 9.

10. Spink, *National Game*, 9; Ryczek, *When Johnny Came Sliding Home*, 51, 206, 220–23; *Chicago Tribune*, May 7 and 8, 1870.

11. Ryczek, *When Johnny Came Sliding Home*, 222–23.

12. *Chicago Tribune*, October 14, 1870; Spink, *National Game*, 64.

13. Michael Benson, *Ballparks of North America: A Comprehensive Historical Reference to Baseball Grounds, Yards, and Stadiums, 1845 to Present* (Jefferson, N.C.: McFarland, 1989), 80; *Chicago Tribune*, October 14, 1870.

14. *Chicago Tribune*, December 25, 1870; *Chicago Tribune*, May 6, 1870.

15. Spink, *National Game*, 64: Chicago beat Cincinnati 10–6 on September 7, then again 16–13 on October 13; *Chicago Tribune*, October 14, 1870; Randy Roberts and Carson Cunningham, *Before the Curse: The Chicago Cubs' Glory Years, 1870–1945* (Champaign: University of Illinois Press, 2012), 13–16.

16. *Chicago Tribune*, October 15, 1870.

17. Cunningham, *Before the Curse*, 14.

18. Benson, *Ballparks of North America*, 80; Ryczek, *When Johnny Came Sliding Home*, 229–31; *Chicago Tribune*, December 12, 1870; *Chicago Tribune*, November 12, 1870; *Chicago Tribune*, November 4, 1870.

19. *Chicago Tribune*, October 14, 1870; Voigt, *Baseball: An Illustrated History*, 33–34; Spink, *National Game*, 8; Spalding, *America's National Game*, 141; Ryczek, *When Johnny Came Sliding Home*, 228–29; Cunningham, *Before the Curse*, 15.

20. Spalding, *America's National Game*, 159–60.

21. Federal Writers' Project, *Baseball in Old Chicago*, 11.

22. *Chicago Tribune*, January 17, 1871.

CHAPTER 4. THE PHOENIX

1. Voigt, *Baseball: An Illustrated History*, 36.

2. Spalding, *America's National Game*, 160.

3. Spink, *National Game*, 65, Benson, *Ballparks of North America*, 80.

4. Spink, *National Game*, 65, Benson, *Ballparks of North America*, 80.

5. Marshall Wright, *Nineteenth Century Baseball: Year-by-Year Statistics for the Major League Teams, 1871 through 1900* (Jefferson, N.C.: McFarland, 1996), 8.

6. Voigt, *Baseball: An Illustrated History*, 40, 57; Spink, *National Game*, 65; Benson, *Ballparks of North America*, 80.

7. *Chicago Tribune*, October 8, 1871.

8. *Chicago Tribune*, October 14, 1871.

9. *Chicago Tribune*, October 18, 1871.

10. Ibid.

11. Ibid.; *Chicago Tribune,* November 3, 1871.

12. *Chicago Tribune,* November 10, 1871; Spalding, *America's National Game,* 168; Federal Writers' Project, *Baseball in Old Chicago,* 26; Wright, *Nineteenth Century Baseball,* 8; Voigt, *Baseball: An Illustrated History,* 40; *Chicago Tribune,* November 3, 1871; *Chicago Tribune,* November 5, 1871.

13. *Chicago Tribune,* November 13, 1871.

14. Federal Writers' Project, *Baseball in Old Chicago,* 26–27.

15. See team listings in Spalding, *America's National Game,* 161–63; Spalding, *America's National Game,* 167; Wright, *Nineteenth Century Baseball,* 8–28; the *Chicago Tribune* of October 8, 1876 confirms the hiatus, and so does the *Chicago Tribune* of May 7, 1874, which refers to the first game by a Chicago professional team since 1871.

16. *Chicago Tribune,* April 8 and April 14, 1872; John Moses and Joseph Kirkland, *History of Chicago, Ill., Vol. 2* (Chicago: Munsell, 1895), 45.

17. *Chicago Tribune,* April 5, May 5, and May 30, 1872.

18. *Chicago Tribune,* July 19 and 20, 1873.

19. *Chicago Tribune,* April 5 and May 14, 1874.

20. Wright, *Nineteenth Century Baseball,* 28.

21. Federal Writers' Project, *Baseball in Old Chicago,* 27, Benson, *Ballparks of North America,* 81, Spalding, *America's National Game,* 169.

22. Spalding, *America's National Game,* 169.

23. Voigt, *Baseball: An Illustrated History,* 37, Spalding, *America's National Game,* 163–69.

24. John Rosenburg, *They Gave Us Baseball: The 12 Extraordinary Men Who Shaped the Major Leagues* (Mechanicsburg, Pa.: Stackpole Books, 1989), 15; Voigt, *Baseball: An Illustrated History,* 50.

CHAPTER 5. CHICAGO'S OWN LEAGUE

1. Hulbert Family Papers, manuscript, Chicago History Museum. Letter to Eri Hulbert, May 24, 1875.

2. Hulbert Family Papers, manuscript, Chicago History Museum. Letter to Ethelyn Hulbert, July 2, 1875.

3. Spalding, *America's National Game,* 169.

4. *New York Times,* March 22, 1875.

5. *Chicago Tribune,* June 27, 1875, 14; *Chicago Tribune,* February 27, 1876.

6. Rosenburg, *They Gave Us Baseball,* 17.

7. Although in 1871, the year of the incorporation of the Chicago White Stockings, the National Association had had a strong western contingent—with Chicago, Cleveland, Rockford, and Fort Wayne (the latter disbanded in July)—by 1874 Chi-

cago was the only team not hailing from the eastern seaboard. In 1875, four of the thirteen teams were from the West. For a list of teams active in the league in the early 1870s, see Spalding, *America's National Game*, 159–72.

8. Spalding, *America's National Game*, 201.

9. Voigt, *Baseball: An Illustrated History*, 52; Wright, *Nineteenth Century Baseball*, 13, 28–41; Rucker and Freyer, *19th Century Baseball in Chicago*, 24.

10. Spalding, *America's National Game*, 204.

11. Adrian Anson, *A Ball Player's Career: Being the Personal Experiences and Reminiscences of Adrian C. Anson* (Chicago: Era Publishing, 1900), 92.

12. Ibid., 41.

13. Ibid., 7, 9.

14. Ibid., 41–43.

15. Ibid., 31–32, 52.

16. Ibid., 69, 78.

17. Ibid., 92; Wright, *Nineteenth Century Baseball*, 14, 21, 27, 33.

18. Spalding, *America's National Game*, 208.

19. Voigt, *Baseball: An Illustrated History*, 52.

20. Spalding, *America's National Game*, 211.

21. Ibid.

22. Ibid., 519–21; Anson, *Ball Player's Career*, 93.

23. H. G. Fisher, *1910–11 Spalding's Official Chicago Base Ball Guide* (Chicago: A.G. Spalding, 1910), 8; Names, *Bury My Heart*, 118.

24. Federal Writers' Project, *Baseball in Old Chicago*, 29; Spink, *National Game*, 12; Spalding, *America's National Game*, 219.

CHAPTER 6. THE BIRTH OF A DYNASTY

1. Benson, *Ballparks of North America*, 81; Chicago Cubs cash book, 1876–1881, Chicago History Museum; *Chicago Tribune*, April 2, 1876.

2. Art Ahrens, Eddie Gold, and John Warner Davenport, *The Cubs: The Complete Record of Chicago Cubs Baseball* (New York: Collier Books, 1986, 23.

3. *Chicago Tribune*, September 17, 1876.

4. Federal Writers' Project, *Baseball in Old Chicago*, 30.

5. *Chicago Inter Ocean*, October 23, 1876.

6. *Chicago Tribune*, September 17, 1876.

7. Ahrens, Gold, and Davenport, *Chicago Cubs Baseball*, 25.

8. Federal Writers' Project, *Baseball in Old Chicago*, 37.

9. Peter Levine, *A.G. Spalding and the Rise of Baseball: The Promise of American Sport* (New York: Oxford University Press, 1986), 71–77.

10. Benson, *Ballparks of North America*, 81, 82.

11. Steven Riess, *Touching Base: Professional Baseball and America Culture in the Progressive Era* (Westport, Conn.: Greenwood Press, 1980), 101.

12. Levine, *A.G. Spalding*, 36.

13. Chicago Cubs cash book, 1876–1881, Chicago History Museum.

14. Ibid.

15. Federal Writers' Project, *Baseball in Old Chicago*, 37.

16. Ahrens, Gold, and Davenport, *Chicago Cubs Baseball*, 27.

17. Chicago Cubs cash book, 1876–1881, Chicago History Museum.

18. Ahrens, Gold, and Davenport, *Chicago Cubs Baseball*, 29.

19. Federal Writers' Project, *Baseball in Old Chicago*, 41, Ahrens, Gold, and Davenport, *Chicago Cubs Baseball*, 31.

20. Spalding, *America's National Game*, 265.

21. *Chicago Tribune*, September 16, 1880.

22. *Chicago Tribune*, October 1 and 2, 1880.

23. Ahrens, Gold, and Davenport, *Chicago Cubs Baseball*, 33.

24. Randy Roberts and Carson Cunningham, *Before the Curse: The Chicago Cubs' Glory Years, 1870–1945* (Champaign: University of Illinois Press, 2012), 18–20.

25. *Chicago Tribune*, October 1, 1882.

26. *Chicago Tribune*, October 2, 1882.

27. *Chicago Tribune*, October 11–13, October 17, and October 20–25, 1882.

28. *Chicago Tribune*, October 27, 1882.

29. National League Ball Club records, Chicago History Museum, Attendance ledger; Benson, *Ballparks of North America*, 82; *Harper's Weekly*, May 12, 1883, 299.

30. Ahrens, Gold, and Davenport, *Chicago Cubs Baseball*, 37.

31. National League Ball Club records, Chicago History Museum, attendance ledger.

32. Federal Writers' Project, *Baseball in Old Chicago*, 43; Anson, *Ball Player's Career*, 128.

33. Ahrens, Gold, and Davenport, *Chicago Cubs Baseball*, 39; *Chicago Tribune*, October 1–5, 1884.

34. Donald Honig, *The Chicago Cubs: An Illustrated History* (New York: Prentice Hall, 1991), 7–8; Benson, *Ballparks of North America*, 83.

35. National League Ball Club records, Chicago History Museum, attendance ledger.

36. Riess, *Touching Base*, 111, note 3.

CHAPTER 7. KEEPING THE STOCKINGS WHITE

1. Levine, *A.G. Spalding,* 47.

2. Glenn Dickey, *The History of National League Baseball: Since 1876* (New York: Stein & Day, 1982), 154.

3. Ibid., 36.

4. Phil Mullen and Mark Clark, "Blacks in Baseball: An Historical Perspective, 1867–1988," in *Cooperstown: Symposium on Baseball and American Culture* (Westport, Conn.: Meckler, 1989), 126.

5. Leslie Heaphy, *The Negro Leagues, 1869–1960* (Jefferson, N.C.: McFarland, 2003), 14.

6. Ibid., 11, 14.

7. Mullen and Clark, "Blacks in Baseball," 124–25.

8. Levine, *A.G. Spalding,* 101.

9. Mary Beth Norton et al., *A People and a Nation: Volume II: Since 1865* (Boston: Houghton Mifflin, 1986), 460, 490.

10. Heaphy, *Negro Leagues,* 4.

11. Mullen and Clark, "Blacks in Baseball," 123; Heaphy, *Negro Leagues,* 10.

12. Heaphy, *Negro Leagues,* 11.

13. Ibid., 13.

14. Ibid., 13–14.

15. Mullen and Clark, "Blacks in Baseball," 125.

16. Ibid., 124.

17. Ibid., 126.

18. Dickey, *National League Baseball,* 154; Jerry Malloy, "Rube Foster and Black Baseball in Chicago," in *Baseball in Chicago* (Chicago: Regional Chapter of the Society for American Baseball Research, 1986), 24.

19. Voigt, *Baseball: An Illustrated History,* 279.

20. Malloy, "Rube Foster," 24–25; Benson, *Ballparks of North America,* 93.

21. Heaphy, *Negro Leagues,* 39–40.

CHAPTER 8. WEST SIDE HOME

1. *The Mirror of American Sports,* June 6, 1885; Robinsons' Atlas of Chicago, 1886, vol. 4, plate 7; Benson, *Ballparks of North America,* 85.

2. U.S. Census Office, 11th Census, 1890, #18, Transportation and Business, part 1, Transportation by Land, 702.

3. Benson, *Ballparks of North America,* 85.

4. Spink, *National Game,* 64.

5. U.S. Census office, Report on Vital and Social Statistics in the United States

at the 11th Census: 1890, part 2, Vital Statistics, Cities of 100,000 Population and Upward, 167, 171, 172.

6. *Mirror of American Sports,* June 6, 1885.

7. Freedman, "Baseball Fad in Chicago," 50.

8. Riess, *Touching Base,* 159.

9. Spalding, *America's National Game,* 5.

10. *Mirror of American Sports,* June 6, 1885.

11. Carter H. Harrison, "A Kentucky Colony," in Caroline Kirkland, *Chicago Yesterdays: A Sheaf of Reminiscences* (Chicago: Daughaday, 1919), 162. Carter H. Harrison Sr. was mayor from 1879 to 1887 and again briefly in 1893 before being assassinated.

12. U.S. Census Office, Report on Vital and Social Statistics in the United States at the 11th Census: 1890, part 2, Vital Statistics, Cities of 100,000 Population and Upward, 167.

13. Ibid., 172.

14. Ibid., 171.

15. *Sunday Herald,* October 4, 1885.

16. *Chicago Tribune,* September 30, 1885; Kuhn scrapbooks, CHS.

17. *Chicago Daily Inter Ocean,* September 30, 1885.

18. *Chicago Inter Ocean,* October 1, 1885, Kuhn scrapbooks, CHS.

19. Ahrens, Gold, and Warner, *Chicago Cubs Baseball,* 41.

20. Federal Writers' Project, *Baseball in Old Chicago,* 43; Anson, *Ball Player's Career,* 128.

21. Reported in unmarked September 17, 1885 article, Kuhn scrapbooks, CHS.

22. *Chicago Daily Inter Ocean,* October 3, 1885, Kuhn scrapbooks, CHS.

23. Anson, *Ball Player's Career,* 124.

24. *Chicago Daily Inter Ocean,* October 7, 1885, Kuhn scrapbooks, CHS.

25. Ibid., October 8, 1885.

CHAPTER 9. THE NATIONAL LEAGUE AIN'T THE WORLD

1. Gary Hailey, "The Business of Baseball," *SABR Review of Books* 4 (1989): 23.

2. Anson, *Ball Player's Career,* 288.

3. Voigt, *Baseball: An Illustrated History,* 12–13.

4. Federal Writers' Project, *Baseball in Old Chicago,* 51.

5. Levine, *A.G. Spalding,* 34–35; Voigt, *Baseball: An Illustrated History,* 140.

6. *Chicago Inter Ocean,* Kuhn scrapbooks, Chicago History Museum.

7. Anson, *Ball Player's Career,* 136; Ahrens, Gold, and Davenport, *Chicago Cubs Baseball,* 41.

8. Ahrens, Gold, and Davenport, *Chicago Cubs Baseball,* 43; Derek Gentile, *The*

Complete Chicago Cubs: The Total Encyclopedia of the Team (New York: Black Dog & Leventhal, 2002), 17–18, 702.

9. National League Club records, Chicago History Museum: attendance.

10. Anson, *Ball Player's Career,* 137.

11. Lewis Meacham, *Spalding's Base Ball Guide and Official League Book, 1886* (New York: Spalding's Athletic Library, 1886), 7, 29.

CHAPTER 10. THE SABBATH BATTLES

1. Riess, *Touching Base,* 121.

2. Hulbert's 1870s crackdown included banning alcohol from the parks. See Spink, *National Game,* 18, and Spalding, *America's National Game,* 219.

3. *Chicago Tribune,* October 7, 1880.

4. *Chicago Evening Journal,* April 30, 1887, quoted in Riess, *Touching Base,* 144, note 4.

5. Spalding, *America's National Game,* 241.

6. Ibid., 257.

7. Levine, *A.G. Spalding,* 44.

8. Riess, *Touching Base,* 123.

9. Letter to President of South Division, Rail Road, January 11, 1890, National League Club records, Chicago History Museum; Benson, *Ballparks of North America,* 86; Riess, *Touching Base,* 86.

10. David L. Fleitz, *Cap Anson: The Grand Old Man of Baseball* (Jefferson, N.C.: McFarland, 2005), 236.

11. Riess, *Touching Base,* 123.

12. Benson, *Ballparks of North America,* 87; Riess, *Touching Base,* 123.

13. National League Club records, Chicago History Museum: attendance.

14. Art Ahrens, "How the Cubs Got Their Name," *Chicago History* (Spring 1976): 41; Spink, *National Game,* 66.

15. Riess, *Touching Base,* 123.

16. Stanley Applebaum, *The Chicago World's Fair of 1893* (Mineola, N.Y.: Dover Publications, 1980), 6, 103.

17. Riess, *Touching Base,* 124.

18. *Chicago Tribune,* June 24, 1895.

19. Ibid., July 10, 1895.

20. Ibid.

21. Ibid., July 21, 1897, 5.

22. Ibid., July 22, 1895, 4. The word *fans* begins to appear around this time in newspaper accounts of games, usually used in quotes. See *Chicago Tribune,* August 19, 1895, 5.

23. *Chicago Tribune,* August 4, 1895, 4.

24. Riess, *Touching Base,* 124.

25. Proceedings of the City Council, 1894–1895: 707, 709, 1819, 1950, 2314; 1895–1896: 2395.

CHAPTER 11. "IT WAS STRAIGHT WHISKEY"

1. Riess, *Touching Base,* 86, Benson, *Ballparks of North America,* 85.

2. Riess, *Touching Base,* 86.

3. 12th Census of the United States, 1900, Vol. 1, Population, 116; 13th Census of United States, 1910, Abstract with Supplement for Illinois, 644–45; U.S. Census Office, Report on Vital and Social Statistics in the United States at the 11th Census: 1890, part 2, Vital Statistics, Cities of 100,000 Population and Upward, 167, 171, 172.

4. Spalding, *America's National Game,* 522–26.

5. Levine, *A.G. Spalding,* 43.

6. Benson, *Ballparks of North America,* 86; Riess, *Touching Base,* 101.

7. Riess, *Touching Base,* 86, 103.

8. *Chicago Herald,* October 5, 1885.

9. Sunday, quoted in Spalding, *America's National Game,* 440–41; the play sounds very much like one described in the *Chicago Daily News* on August, 8 1887, though such details as the name of the batter differ. It is possible that Sunday, who was quoted on the play in 1904, may have gotten some of the specifics wrong and that the 1887 game was the game in question (see chapter 18).

10. Ibid., 441.

11. Christian Messenger, *Sport and the Spirit of Play in American Fiction* (New York: Columbia University Press, 1981), 330.

12. Roberts and Cunningham, *Before the Curse,* 67.

CHAPTER 12. "MIGHTY CASEY HAS STRUCK OUT"

1. Levine, *A.G. Spalding,* 40–41.

2. Anson, *Ball Player's Career,* 137.

3. Spalding, *America's National Game,* 516.

4. Roberts and Cunningham, *Before the Curse,* 57–58.

5. Ahrens, Gold, and Davenport, *Chicago Cubs Baseball,* 343.

6. Federal Writers' Project, *Baseball in Old Chicago,* 44.

7. Ibid., 44.

8. Ibid., 45.

9. James Mote, *Everything Baseball* (New York: Prentice Hall, 1989), 350, 352.

10. Roberts and Cunningham, *Before the Curse,* 56.

11. Federal Writers' Project, *Baseball in Old Chicago*, 43; Mote, *Everything Baseball*, 350; Roberts and Cunningham, *Before the Curse*, 49.

12. Federal Writers' Project, *Baseball in Old Chicago*, 64.

13. Ibid., 43.

14. Spalding, *America's National Game*, 516–17.

15. Ibid., 526.

16. Ahrens, Gold, and Davenport, *Chicago Cubs Baseball*, 45; Ahrens, *Cubs Got Their Name*, 41.

17. Ahrens, Gold, and Davenport, *Chicago Cubs Baseball*, 45; Voigt, *Baseball: An Illustrated History*, 145.

18. Roberts and Cunningham, *Before the Curse*, 55.

19. Anson, *Ball Player's Career*, 138.

20. Spalding, *America's National Game*, 527.

21. National League Club records, Chicago History Museum: attendance; Spalding, *America's National Game*, 528; Levine, *A.G. Spalding*, 37.

22. Levine, *A.G. Spalding*, 40.

23. *Players National League Baseball Guide, 1890* (Chicago: F.H. Brunell, 1890).

24. Roberts and Cunningham, *Before the Curse*, 57.

25. Ibid., 59–63.

CHAPTER 13. BASEBALL MISSIONARIES

1. National League Club records, Chicago History Museum: attendance.

2. Spalding, *America's National Game*, 252–53.

3. Levine, *A.G. Spalding*, 100.

4. Anson, *Ball Player's Career*, 140; Spalding, *America's National Game*, 264.

5. Anson, *Ball Player's Career*, 142.

6. Ibid., 143.

7. Ibid., 144–50; Spalding, *America's National Game*, 253.

8. Levine, *A.G. Spalding*, 103.

9. Roberts and Cunningham, *Before the Curse*, 73.

10. Anson, *Ball Player's Career*, 144–50; Spalding, *America's National Game*, 259; Roberts and Cunningham, *Before the Curse*, 73.

11. Spalding, *America's National Game*, 261.

12. Ibid., 263.

13. Anson, *Ball Player's Career*, 275.

14. Ibid., 283.

15. Roberts and Cunningham, *Before the Curse*, 69; Levine, *A.G. Spalding and the Rise of Baseball*, 108.

CHAPTER 14. THE LEAN YEARS

1. Chicago's record in 1889 was .508. It had been .500 in 1878. Ahrens, Gold, and Davenport, *Chicago Cubs Baseball,* 49, 27.

2. National League Club Records, Chicago History Museum: attendance.

3. Ahrens, Gold, and Davenport, *Chicago Cubs Baseball,* 53, 55.

4. Chicago Cubs Correspondence, January 8 to September 8, 1890, Chicago History Museum.

5. Charles Fountain, *Under the March Sun: The Story of Spring Training* (New York: Oxford University Press, 2009), 11.

6. Benson, *Ballparks of North America,* 86.

7. Spalding, *America's National Game,* 286.

8. Ibid., 288.

9. *Chicago Times,* March 19, 1892, Benson, *Ballparks of North America,* 86.

CHAPTER 15. BACK TO THE WEST SIDE

1. Greg Borzo, *The Chicago L* (Chicago: Arcadia Publishing, 2007), 43, 51.

2. Benson, *Ballparks of North America,* 86.

3. Riess, *Touching Base,* 95; John Snyder, *Cubs Journal: Year by Year & Day by Day with the Chicago Cubs since 1876* (Cincinnati: Clerisy Press, 2005), 81.

4. *Chicago Tribune,* July 18, 1908, 1; *Chicago Tribune,* July 16, 1908, 6.

5. Riess, *Touching Base,* 94, 114, note 24; Snyder, *Cubs Journal,* 99.

6. Art Ahrens, Eddie Gold, and Buck Peden, *Day by Day in Chicago Cubs History* (West Point, N.Y.: Leisure Press, 1982), 18.

7. Riess, *Touching Base,* 54.

8. Benson, *Ballparks of North America,* 85.

9. Levine, *A.G. Spalding,* 73, 80.

10. Federal Writers' Project, *Baseball in Old Chicago,* 54–59; Voigt, *Baseball: An Illustrated History,* 248.

11. Katharine Rogers, *L. Frank Baum: Creator of Oz: A Biography* (New York: St Martin's Press, 2002), 66, 261; Frank Joslyn Baum and Russell MacFall, *To Please a Child* (Chicago: Reilly & Lee, 1961), 84.

12. Dennis Abrams and Kyle Zimmer, *L. Frank Baum* (New York: Chelsea House, 2010), 49.

13. Edith Van Dyne, *Aunt Jane's Nieces and Uncle John* (Chicago: Reilly & Britton, 1911), 41; Baum and MacFall, *To Please a Child,* 230–33.

CHAPTER 16. FROM COLTS TO CUBS

1. Ahrens, Gold, and Davenport, *Chicago Cubs Baseball,* 64–65; Federal Writers' Project, *Baseball in Old Chicago,* 33–34, 36–37.

2. Fleitz, *Cap Anson,* 234–35; *Chicago Tribune,* September 17, 1897.

3. *Chicago Tribune,* September 25, 1897.

4. Ibid., September 17, 1897.

5. *Chicago Tribune,* October 23, 1897; *Chicago Tribune,* November 10, 1897; *Chicago Tribune,* December 18, 1897; *Chicago Tribune,* December 26, 1897; *Chicago Tribune,* January 13, 1898; *Chicago Tribune,* January 24, 1898.

6. Fleitz, *Cap Anson,* 265–69, 270, 272–74, 275–76.

7. Ibid., 282.

8. Ibid., 284–86.

9. Ibid., 287–89.

10. Ibid., 290.

11. Ibid., 293.

12. *Chicago Tribune,* July 17, 1908, 6; Fleitz, *Cap Anson,* 296–98.

13. Fleitz, *Cap Anson,* 296–98.

14. Ibid., 346; John Leonard, *The Book of Chicagoans: A Biographical Dictionary of Leading Men and Women of the City of Chicago* (Chicago: A.N. Marquis, 1905), 23.

15. Mote, *Everything Baseball,* 36–38.

16. Fleitz, *Cap Anson,* 346.

17. The team first held spring training at West Baden, Indiana in 1897 (Frank Chance's tryout was held there in 1898). The team trained there off and on, including during the 1906–1908 World Series seasons and during World War II. In 1908, the Cubs began spring training there before heading south and finishing with a tour of Indiana that included Evansville, Fort Wayne, Terre Haute, and Indianapolis. Roberts and Cunningham, *Before the Curse,* 75–76, 101; John O'Malley, "The Story of the West Baden Springs Hotel," in *Indiana Magazine of History* 54, no. 4 (December 1958), 375; George Matthews, *When the Cubs Won it All: The 1908 Championship Season,* (Jefferson, N.C.: McFarland, 2009), 9.

18. Roberts and Cunningham, *Before the Curse,* 75–76.

19. Honig, *Chicago Cubs,* 18; Ahrendt, "Cubs Got Their Name," 42–43; *Chicago Tribune,* September 26 and 29 and October 6, 1901.

20. Gil Bogen, *Tinker, Evers, and Chance: A Triple Biography* (Jefferson, N.C.: McFarland, 2003), 19–20.

21. Ibid., 24–25.

22. Ibid., 10–13; Gentile, *Complete Chicago Cubs,* 123.

23. Ahrens, *Chicago Cubs Baseball,* 43, 75.

24. Glenn Stout, *The Cubs: The Complete Story of Chicago Cubs Baseball* (New York: Houghton Mifflin, 2007), 5.

CHAPTER 17. THE SADDEST OF POSSIBLE WORDS?

1. Franklin Adams, *In Other Words* (Garden City, N.Y.: Doubleday, Page, 1912), 62.

2. Jim Enright, *Chicago Cubs* (New York: McMillan/McGraw Hill, 1975), 124.

3. Often, authors do so by comparing apples and oranges. As Dickey points out in *National League Baseball,* scorekeeping was erratic, base-running strategy made double plays less likely, and gloves made it much more difficult to catch ground balls. Jim Enright puts the fifty-six double plays in four years in perspective by stating that the 1974 White Sox had fifty-six double plays by their forty-second game and that the Cubs reached that mark by their fifty-fourth game. But he ignores his own statistic that the Cubs as a team churned out an average of ninety-eight double plays per year between 1906 and 1910 (124). Bill Bryson (*The Babe Didn't Point: And other Stories about Iowans in Sports,* Iowa State Press University, 1989) writes that the trio's ability has been "exaggerated" and purports to prove his point by comparing the 1906–1909 teams to the 1949 Philadelphia Athletics (major-league record 217 double plays) and the 1966 Pittsburgh Pirates (215 double plays).

4. Enright, *Chicago Cubs,* 119; Dickey, *National League Baseball,* 67.

5. Quoted in Enright, *Chicago Cubs,* 124.

6. Jerome Holtzman, "How a Poem Helped Elect Infield Trio to Hall of Fame," *Baseball Digest,* March 1993, 70.

7. Selee is usually credited for Chance's switch to first base (see Dickey, 63), but Chance had also played six games at first in 1901 under manager Tom Loftus, while catching thirteen games and playing in the outfield fifty times.

8. Dickey, *National League Baseball,* 65.

9. Ahrens, Gold, and Peden, *Chicago Cubs History,* 1982.

10. Evers only appeared in ninety-nine games in 1905 owing to a hand injury.

11. Tom Simon, *Deadball Stars of the National League* (Dulles, Va.: Potomac Books, 2004), 124.

12. Pete Cava, *Tales From the Cubs Dugout: A Collection of the Greatest Stories Ever Told* (Champaign, Ill.: Sport Publishing, 2002), 213–14.

13. Holtzman, "*How a Poem Helped,*" 70.

14. Bert Sugar, *The Great Baseball Players: From McGraw to Mantle* (Mineola, Minn.: Dover Publications, 2007), 13.

15. Dickey, *National League Baseball,* 62; Sam Riley, *Biographical Dictionary of American Newspaper Columnists* (Westport, Conn.: Greenwood Press, 1995), 3.

16. Double-play and fielding figures and rankings are from *The Baseball Encyclopedia* (individual rankings were compiled by the author from the *Encyclopedia*'s fielding-average figures because players with inferior fielding averages are sometimes mistakenly listed as first in the book's rankings).

17. Snyder, *Cubs Journal,* 130.

18. Ibid., 138.

19. Christy Mathewson, *Pitching in a Pinch: Or Baseball From the Inside* (New York: G.P. Putnam, 1912), 297.

20. Bogen, *Tinker, Evers, and Chance,* 121–23, 137–38; Snyder, *Cubs Journal,* 167, 170; Hugh Fullerton, "The Baseball Primer," *American Magazine,* 1912, 1999.

21. Bogen, *Tinker, Evers, and Chance,* 61.

22. Ibid., 86, 185.

23. John L. Evers and Hugh S. Fullerton, *Touching Second: The Science of Baseball* (Chicago: Reilly & Britton, 1910), 265.

24. Hugh Fullerton, "How to Win Games," *American Magazine,* July 1912, 301.

25. Bogen, *Tinker, Evers, and Chance,* 156, 192, 208, 230–31.

26. Ibid., 178.

27. Snyder, *Cubs Journal,* 175, 180.

28. Bogen, *Tinker, Evers, and Chance,* 169, 205.

29. Snyder, *Cubs Journal,* 215; Bogen, *Tinker, Evers, and Chance,* 184–85.

30. Bogen, *Tinker, Evers, and Chance,* 185, 187; Simon, *Deadball Stars,* 92.

31. Bogen, *Tinker, Evers, and Chance,* 200–202, 203–6, 221–24.

32. Ibid., 222.

CHAPTER 18. "THE FELLOWS WHO MADE THE GAME"

1. Gunther Barth, *City People: The Rise of Modern City Culture in Nineteenth Century America* (New York: Oxford University Press, 1980), 164; Steven Riess and Gerald Gems, *The Chicago Sports Reader: 100 Years of Sports in the Windy City* (Champaign: University of Illinois Press, 2009), 22.

2. Hugh Fullerton, "The Fellows Who Made the Game," *Saturday Evening Post,* April 21, 1928, 18.

3. Alfred Lawrence, "The Whitechapel Club: Defining Chicago's Newspapermen in the 1890s," *American Journalism* 15, no. 1 (Winter 1998): 83–102.

4. Elmer Ellis, *Mr. Dooley's America: A Life of Finley Peter Dunne* (New York: Alfred A. Knopf, 1942), 23; Barbara Schaaf, *Mr. Dooley's Chicago* (Garden City, N.Y.: Anchor Press, 1977), 150; Charles Fanning, *Finley Peter Dunne and Mr. Dooley: The Chicago Years* (La Vergne, Tenn.: Lightning Source, 2008), 8.

5. Ellis, *Mr. Dooley's America,* 27.

6. Schaaf, *Mr. Dooley's Chicago,* 150; Christine Ammer, *Southpaws and Sunday Punches and Other Baseball Expressions* (New York: Penguin Books, 1994), 206; Paul Dickson, *The Dickson Baseball Dictionary* (New York: W.W. Norton, 2009), 806.

7. Dickson, *Dickson Baseball Dictionary,* 805–6.

8. *Oxford English Dictionary,* www.oed.com, retrieved March 16, 2011: The January 14, 1885 *Sporting Life* wrote, "They had always been accustomed to having their opponents hug their bases pretty close, out of respect for Morris' quick throw over to first with that south-paw of his"; John Shiffert, *Baseball in Philadelphia* (Jefferson, N.C.: McFarland, 2006), 243; Riley, *American Newspaper Columnists,* 77–78.

9. Fullerton, "Fellows Who Made the Game," 18.

10. *Chicago Inter Ocean,* July 23, 1880.

11. Roberts and Cunningham, *Before the Curse,* 29–33.

12. *Chicago Herald,* June 21, 1882.

13. *Chicago Inter Ocean,* August 31, 1883.

14. Ibid., August 26, 1885.

15. *Chicago Tribune,* July 7, 1885, quoted in Federal Writers' Project, *Baseball in Old Chicago,* 45.

16. *Chicago Daily News,* October 19, 1886, 1.

17. Ibid., October 22, 1886.

18. Ibid., October 23, 1886.

19. *Chicago Daily News,* August 8, 1887

20. Ellis, *Mr. Dooley's America,* 27; Riley, *American Newspaper Columnists,* 77.

21. *Chicago Herald,* July 16, 1887.

22. Fullerton, "Fellows Who Made the Game," 18–19; *Public Opinion* 12, no. 2 (October 1891): 72.

23. *Chicago Daily News,* September 29, 1887.

24. *Chicago Times,* January 7, 1892, Kuhn scrapbooks, Chicago History Museum.

25. *Chicago Times,* January 15, 1892, Kuhn scrapbooks.

26. George Ade, *Fables in Slang* (Chicago: Herbert Stone, 1899), 47.

27. *Saturday Evening Post,* April 21, 1928, 18; Spink, *National Game,* 350.

28. Messenger, *Sport and the Spirit of Play,* 111.

29. Jonathan Yardley, ed., *Selected Stories, Ring Lardner* (New York: Penguin Books, 1997), i, viii.

30. Messenger, *Sport and the Spirit of Play,* 99, 111.

31. Fullerton, "Fellows Who Made the Game," 18.

CHAPTER 19. OUT IN LEFT FIELD?

1. Maggie Sokolik, "Out of Left Field: Baseball and American Idiom," Cooperstown Symposium on Baseball and the American Culture (Westport, Conn.: Meckler, 1989), 85–99.

2. *Washington Post* and *Charleston News and Courier,* quoted in Sokolik, "Out of Left Field," 85; see also Barth, *Rise of Modern City Culture,* 164.

3. William Safire, *I Stand Corrected* (New York: Times Books, 1984), 232.

4. J. M. Mosher, M.D., "The Insane in General Hospitals," *Proceedings of the American Medico-Psychological Association,* 1900, 150; *Chicago Daily News Almanac and Year Book,* 1903, 376; "Annual Report Cook County Detention Hospital," Cook County Charity Work During the Year 1903, December 1, 1903, 58; "The Chicago Meeting of Alienists and Neurologists," *Institution Quarterly* 5, no. 3 (September 30, 1914): 14; "New Psychopathic Hospital for Chicago Marks New Era," *Institution Quarterly* 5, no. 4 (December 31, 1914): 94.

5. Dickson, *Dickson Baseball Dictionary,* 612–13; Safire, *I Stand Corrected,* 234–35.

6. Ammer, *Southpaws and Sunday Punches,* 157.

7. Safire, *I Stand Corrected,* vii.

8. Phone conversation with the author, March 17, 2011.

9. Dickson, *Dickson Baseball Dictionary,* 2009, 613.

10. "Great Days Coming for the Medics," *Alumni Quarterly and Fortnightly Notes of the University of Illinois Alumni Association* 5, no. 3 (November 1, 1919): 29; Alice Sinkevitch, *AIA Guide to Chicago* (Orlando, Fla.: Harcourt Books, 2004), 294; Eileen Tanner, *The Historical Medical Campus at the University of Illinois at Chicago: History and Self-Guided Tour of the Oldest Buildings and Grounds at UIC* (Chicago: University of Illinois at Chicago, 2012), 37–84.

11. Safire, *I Stand Corrected,* 234–35.

12. Dickson, *Dickson Baseball Dictionary,* 612–13; Safire, *I Stand Corrected,* 234–35; Ammer, *Southpaws and Sunday Punches,* 158.

13. "About New York; On Baseball, Too, A Maven Seeks the Last Word," *New York Times,* October 17, 1990; "A Man of Many Words, David Shulman Dies at 91," *New York Times,* November 7, 2004.

14. See endnote 15.

15. David Kahn, the author of several books on code breaking and military intelligence who was Shulman's friend for more than fifty years, said in an e-mail exchange with the author of this book, "He is unquestionably your man. I don't know about the items you mention, but the letter to Safire sounds like something Dave would have done." (e-mail correspondence, March 17, 2011); Robert Hendrickson, ed.,

New Yawk Tawk: A Dictionary of New York City Expressions (New York: Checkmark Books, 2002), 192, also mentions the Babe Ruth theory, but it does not cite a source, though its wording mirrors Shulman's letter almost exactly.

16. Bill Jenkinson, *The Year Babe Ruth Hit 104 Home Runs: Recrowning Baseball's Greatest Slugger* (New York: Carroll & Graf, 2007), 340–59.

CHAPTER 20. AGAIN, CHICAGO IS CHAMPION

1. Jim Enright, *Chicago Cubs* (New York: McMillan/McGraw Hill, 1975), 12.
2. Ibid., 38.
3. Ahrens, Gold, and Davenport, *Chicago Cubs Baseball,* 76–83.
4. David Sloan and Lisa Parcell, *American Journalism: History, Principles, Practices* (Jefferson, N.C.: McFarland, 2002), 200.
5. Roberts and Cunningham, *Before the Curse,* 84.
6. Joseph Krueger, *Baseball's Greatest Drama: World Series History, 1903–1942,* (Milwaukee, Wisc.: Classic Publishing, 1942), 11–13.
7. Warren Brown, *The Chicago Cubs* (Carbondale: Southern Illinois University Press, 1946), 251.
8. *Chicago Tribune,* October 9, 1906; *Chicago Tribune,* October 10, 1906.
9. *Chicago Tribune,* October 11, 1906
10. Dennis Bingham, "A Fan's-Eye View of the 1906 World Series," in *Baseball in Chicago* (Chicago: Regional Chapter of the Society for American Baseball Research, 1986), 10; *Chicago Tribune,* October 12, 1906.
11. *Chicago Tribune,* October 13, 1906.
12. *Chicago Tribune,* October 14, 1906.
13. Honig, *Chicago Cubs,* 31–32; Bingham, "Fan's-Eye," 5–10, 48–52; Riess, *Touching Base,* 54; Enright, *Chicago Cubs,* 39–40; Brown, *Chicago Cubs,* 41; Roberts and Cunningham, *Before the Curse,* 96; *Chicago Tribune,* October 15, 1906.
14. Hugh Fullerton, "Fans," American Magazine, 1912, vol. 72, 462.
15. Lewis Meacham, *Spalding's Official Base Ball Guide 1907* (New York: A.G. Spalding, 1907).
16. Ray Schmidt, "The Semi-Pro Team that Beat the Champs," in *Baseball in Chicago,* 22–23.

CHAPTER 21. COVERING THE BASES

1. Proceedings of the City Council, October 8, 1906, 1428–29.
2. National League Ball Club's records, Chicago History Museum.
3. Riess, *Touching Base,* 53–54.
4. Proceedings of the City Council, 1906, 291.

5. September 16, 1885, letter, National League Ball Club Correspondence, Chicago History Museum.

6. Steven Riess and Gerald Gems, ed., *The Chicago Sports Reader: 100 Years of Sports in the Windy City* (Champaign: University of Illinois Press, 2009), 199.

7. Riess, *Touching Base,* 56.

8. Roberts and Cunningham, *Before the Curse,* 81.

CHAPTER 22. THREE MORE PENNANTS

1. Ahrens, Gold, and Davenport, *Chicago Cubs Baseball,* 85, Brown, *Chicago Cubs,* 44–45.

2. Bogen, *Tinker, Evers, and Chance,* 63, 76 and 103; Simon, *Deadball Stars,* 92; *Chicago Tribune,* October 6, 1912.

3. Bruce Rubenstein, *Chicago in the World Series, 1903–2005* (Jefferson, N.C.: McFarland,

2006), 22.

4. Ahrens, Gold, and Davenport, *Chicago Cubs Baseball,* 85, Spink, *National Game,* 68, Honig, *Chicago Cubs,* 19; Snyder, *Cubs Journal,* 141–42; Gentile, *Complete Chicago Cubs,* 25; *Chicago Tribune,* October 13, 1907.

5. Ahrens, Gold, and Davenport, *Chicago Cubs Baseball,* 87.

6. Evers, *Touching Second,* 187.

7. Roberts and Cunningham, *Before the Curse,* 119–20.

8. *Chicago Tribune,* October 5, 1908; Snyder, *Cubs Journal,* 148–49.

9. Voigt, *Baseball: An Illustrated History,* 37; Enright, *Chicago Cubs,* 62–66; Dickey, *National League Baseball,* 68–71; John Evers and Hugh Fullerton, *Touching Second: The Science of Baseball* (Chicago: Reilly & Britton, 1910), 187; Snyder, *Cubs Journal,* 149.

10. Brown, *Chicago Cubs,* 54–55.

11. *Chicago Daily News,* October 15, 1908.

12. Voigt, *Baseball: An Illustrated History,* 38, Brown, *Chicago Cubs,* 56–59.

13. Snyder, *Cubs Journal,* 158.

14. Ibid.

15. *Chicago Daily News,* October 24, 1910.

16. Voigt, *Baseball: An Illustrated History,* 38; Brown, *Chicago Cubs,* 56–59.

17. Snyder, *Cubs Journal,* 164.

18. Riess, *City Games,* 197, *Chicago Tribune,* October 13, 1907.

CHAPTER 23. GOING, GOING . . .

1. Ahrens, Gold, and Davenport, *Chicago Cubs Baseball,* 93.

2. Snyder, *Cubs Journal,* 166.

3. Ahrens, Gold, and Davenport, *Chicago Cubs Baseball,* 93–98.

4. Bogen, *Tinker, Evers, and Chance,* 123–25; Snyder, *Cubs Journal,* 173.

5. Simon, *Deadball Stars,* 92.

6. *Chicago Tribune,* October 6, 1912.

7. Ahrens, Gold, and Davenport, *Chicago Cubs Baseball,* 93–98; Snyder, *Cubs Journal,* 171, 175; Roberts and Cunningham, *Before the Curse,* 149–51.

8. Ahrens, Gold, and Davenport, *Chicago Cubs Baseball,* 99.

9. *Chicago Tribune,* October 4, 1915, 13.

10. *Chicago Tribune,* October 9, 10, and 11, 1915; Brown, *Chicago Cubs,* 251.

CHAPTER 24. GONE

1. Richard Lindberg, "The Chicago Whales and the Federal League of American Baseball, 1914–1915," *Chicago History* (Spring 1981): 3–12; Voigt, *Baseball: An Illustrated History,* 118–19.

2. Ibid.

3. *Chicago Tribune,* October 24, 1919.

4. Lindberg, "Chicago Whales," 3–12; Voigt, *Baseball: An Illustrated History,* 118–19.

5. Snyder, *Cubs Journal,* 173–74.

6. Benson, *Ballparks of North America,* 93; Paul Michael Peterson, *Chicago's Wrigley Field* (Charleston, S.C.: Arcadia Publishing, 2005), 15.

BIBLIOGRAPHY

Abrams, Dennis. *L. Frank Baum*. New York: Chelsea House, 2010.

Adams, Franklin. *In Other Words*. Garden City, N.Y.: Doubleday, Page, 1912.

Ade, George and Clyde Newman. *Fables in Slang*. Chicago: Herbert Stone, 1899.

Ahrens, Art. "How the Cubs Got Their Name." *Chicago History* (Spring 1976).

Ahrens, Art, Eddie Gold, and John Warner Davenport. *The Cubs: The Complete Record of Chicago Cubs Baseball*. New York: Collier Books, 1986.

Ahrens, Art, Eddie Gold, and Buck Peden. *Day by Day in Chicago Cubs History*. West Point, N.Y.: Leisure Press, 1982.

Ammer, Christine. *Southpaws and Sunday Punches and Other Baseball Expressions*. New York: Penguin Books, 1994.

"Annual Report: Cook County Detention Hospital." *Cook County Charity Work During the Year 1903*, December 1, 1903.

Anson, Adrian. *A Ball Player's Career: Being the Personal Experiences and Reminiscences of Adrian C. Anson*. Chicago: Era Publishing, 1900.

Appel, Marty. *The First Book of Baseball*. New York: Crown Publishers, 1990.

Applebaum, Stanley. *The Chicago World's Fair of 1893*. Mineola, N.Y.: Dover Publications, 1980.

Barth, Gunther. *City People: The Rise of Modern City Culture in Nineteenth Century America*. New York: Oxford University Press, 1980.

Baum, Frank Joslyn, and Russell MacFall. *To Please a Child*. Chicago: Reilly & Lee, 1961.

Benson, Michael. *Ballparks of North America: A Comprehensive Historical Reference to Baseball Grounds, Yards, and Stadiums, 1845 to Present*. Jefferson, N.C.: McFarland, 1989.

Bingham, Dennis. "A Fan's-Eye View of the 1906 World Series." In *Baseball in Chicago*. Chicago: Regional Chapter of the Society for American Baseball Research, 1986.

Bogen, Gil. *Tinker, Evers, and Chance: A Triple Biography*. Jefferson, N.C.: McFarland, 2003.

Borzo, Greg. *The Chicago L*. Chicago: Arcadia Publishing, 2007.

Brown, Warren. *The Chicago Cubs*. Carbondale: Southern Illinois University Press, 1946.

Bryson, Bill. *The Babe Didn't Point: And Other Stories about Iowans and Sports*. Iowa City: Iowa State University Press, 1989.

Cava, Pete. *Tales From the Cubs Dugout: A Collection of the Greatest Stories Ever Told*. Champaign, Ill.: Sport Publishing, 2002.

Chadwick, Henry. *The Game of Baseball: How to Learn It, How to Play It, and How to Teach It*. New York: George Munro, 1868.

Chicago Daily News Almanac and Year Book, 1903.

"The Chicago Meeting of Alienists and Neurologists." *Institution Quarterly* 5, no. 3 (September 30, 1914).

Dickey, Glenn. *The History of National League Baseball: Since 1876*. New York: Stein & Day, 1982.

Dickson, Paul. *The Dickson Baseball Dictionary*. New York: W.W. Norton, 2009.

Ellis, Elmer. *Mr. Dooley's America: A Life of Finley Peter Dunne*. New York: Alfred A. Knopf, 1942.

Enright, Jim. *Chicago Cubs*. New York: McMillan/McGraw Hill, 1975.

Evers, John, and Hugh Fullerton. *Touching Second: The Science of Baseball*. Chicago: Reilly & Britton, 1910.

Fanning, Charles. *Finley Peter Dunne and Mr. Dooley: The Chicago Years*. La Vergne, Tenn.: Lightning Source, 2008.

Federal Writers' Project (Illinois), Works Progress Administration. *Baseball in Old Chicago*. Chicago: A.C. McClurg, 1939.

Fisher, H. G., ed. *1910–11 Spalding's Official Chicago Base Ball Guide*. Chicago: A.G. Spalding, 1910.

Fleitz, David L. *Cap Anson: The Grand Old Man of Baseball*. Jefferson, N.C.: McFarland, 2005.

Fountain, Charles. *Under the March Sun: The Story of Spring Training*. New York: Oxford University Press, 2009.

Freedman, Stephen. "The Baseball Fad in Chicago, 1865–1870: An Exploration of the Role of Sport in the Nineteenth-Century City." *Journal of Sport History* (Summer 1978).

Fullerton, Hugh. "The Baseball Primer." *American Magazine,* July 1912.

——. "The Fellows Who Made the Game." *Saturday Evening Post,* April 21, 1928.

——. "How to Win Games." *American Magazine,* July 1912.

Gentile, Derek. *The Complete Chicago Cubs: The Total Encyclopedia of the Team.* New York: Black Dog & Leventhal, 2002.

Goldstein, Warren. *Playing for Keeps: A History of Early Baseball.* Ithaca, N.Y.: Cornell University Press, 1989.

"Great Days Coming for the Medics." *Alumni Quarterly and Fortnightly Notes of the University of Illinois Alumni Association* 5, no. 3 (November 1, 1919).

Hailey, Gary. "The Business of Baseball." *SABR Review of Books* 4 (1989).

Heaphy, Leslie. *The Negro Leagues, 1869–1960.* Jefferson, N.C.: McFarland, 2003.

Hendrickson, Robert, ed. *New Yawk Tawk: A Dictionary of New York City Expressions.* New York: Checkmark Books, 2002.

Holtzman, Jerome. "How a Poem Helped Elect Infield Trio to Hall of Fame." *Baseball Digest,* March 1993.

Honig, Donald. *The Chicago Cubs: An Illustrated History.* New York: Prentice Hall, 1991.

Jenkinson, Bill. *The Year Babe Ruth Hit 104 Home Runs: Recrowning Baseball's Greatest Slugger.* New York: Carroll & Graf, 2007.

Kirkland, Caroline. *Chicago Yesterdays: A Sheaf of Reminiscences.* Chicago: Daughaday, 1919.

Kirsch, George. *Baseball in Blue and Gray: The National Pastime During the Civil War.* Princeton, N.J.: Princeton University Press, 2003.

Krueger, Joseph. *Baseball's Greatest Drama: World Series History, 1903–1942.* Milwaukee, Wisc.: Classic Publishing, 1942.

Leonard, John, ed. *The Book of Chicagoans: A Biographical Dictionary of Leading Men and Women of the City of Chicago.* Chicago: A.N. Marquis, 1905.

Levine, Peter. *A.G. Spalding and the Rise of Baseball: The Promise of American Sport.* New York: Oxford University Press, 1986.

Lindberg, Richard. "The Chicago Whales and the Federal League of American Baseball, 1914–1915." *Chicago History* (Spring 1981).

Lorenz, Alfred Lawrence. "The Whitechapel Club: Defining Chicago's Newspapermen in the 1890s." *American Journalism* 15, no. 1 (Winter 1998).

Malloy, Jerry. "Rube Foster and Black Baseball in Chicago." In *Baseball in Chicago.* Chicago: Regional Chapter of the Society for American Baseball Research, 1986.

Mathewson, Christy. *Pitching in a Pinch: Or Baseball From the Inside.* New York: G.P. Putnam, 1912.

Matthews, George. *When the Cubs Won It All: The 1908 Championship Season.* Jefferson, N.C.: McFarland, 2009.

Meacham, Lewis, ed. *Spalding's Base Ball Guide and Official League Book, 1886.* New York: A.G. Spalding, 1886.

———. *Spalding's Official Base Ball Guide 1904.* New York: A.G. Spalding, 1904.

———. *Spalding's Official Base Ball Guide 1907.* New York: A.G. Spalding, 1907.

Messenger, Christian. *Sport and the Spirit of Play in American Fiction.* New York: Columbia University Press, 1981.

Moses, John, and Joseph Kirkland. *History of Chicago, Ill., Vol. 2.* Chicago: Munsell, 1895.

Mosher, J. M. "The Insane in General Hospitals." *Proceedings of the American Medico-Psychological Association,* 1900.

Mote, James. *Everything Baseball.* New York: Prentice Hall, 1989.

Mullen, Phil, and Mark Clark. "Blacks in Baseball: An Historical Perspective, 1867–1988." In *Cooperstown: Symposium on Baseball and American Culture,* edited by Alvin L. Hall. Westport, Conn.: Meckler, 1989.

Names, Larry. *Bury My Heart at Wrigley Field: The History of the Chicago Cubs.* Neshkoro, Wisc.: Sportsbook Publishing, 1990.

"New Psychopathic Hospital for Chicago Marks New Era." *Institution Quarterly* 5, no. 4 (December 31, 1914).

Norton, Mary Beth, et al. *A People and a Nation: Volume II: Since 1865.* Boston: Houghton Mifflin, 1986.

Okrent, Daniel, and Harris Lewine. *The Ultimate Baseball Book.* Boston: Houghton Mifflin, 1984.

O'Malley, John. "The Story of the West Baden Springs Hotel." *Indiana Magazine of History* 54, no. 4 (December 1958).

Peterson, Paul Michael. *Chicago's Wrigley Field.* Charleston, S.C.: Arcadia Publishing, 2005.

Players National League Baseball Guide, 1890. Chicago: F.H. Brunell, 1889.

Rader, Benjamin. *Baseball: A History of America's Game.* Champaign: University of Illinois Press, 2008.

Riess, Steven. *City Games: The Evolution of American Urban Society and the Rise of Sports.* Champaign: University of Illinois Press, 1991.

———. *Touching Base: Professional Baseball and America Culture in the Progressive Era.* Westport, Conn.: Greenwood Press, 1980.

Riess, Steven, and Gerald Gems, ed. *The Chicago Sports Reader: 100 Years of Sports in the Windy City.* Champaign: University of Illinois Press, 2009.

Riley, Sam. *Biographical Dictionary of American Newspaper Columnists.* Westport, Conn.: Greenwood Press, 1995.

Roberts, Randy, and Carson Cunningham. *Before the Curse: The Chicago Cubs' Glory Years, 1870–1945.* Champaign: University of Illinois Press, 2012.

Rogers, Katharine. *L. Frank Baum: Creator of Oz: A Biography*. New York: St Martin's Press, 2002.

Rosenburg, John. *They Gave Us Baseball: The 12 Extraordinary Men Who Shaped the Major Leagues*. Mechanicsburg, Pa.: Stackpole Books, 1989.

Rubenstein, Bruce. *Chicago in the World Series, 1903–2005*. Jefferson, N.C.: McFarland, 2006.

Rucker, Mark, and John Freyer. *19th Century Baseball in Chicago*. Charleston, S.C.: Arcadia Publishing, 2003.

Ryczek, William. *Baseball's First Inning: A History of the National Pastime Through the Civil War*. Jefferson, N.C.: McFarland, 2009.

———. *When Johnny Came Sliding Home: The Post–Civil War Baseball Boom, 1865–1870*. Jefferson, N.C.: McFarland, 2006.

Safire, William. *I Stand Corrected*. New York: Times Books, 1984.

Schaaf, Barbara. *Mr. Dooley's Chicago*. Garden City, N.Y.: Anchor Press, 1977.

Schmidt, Ray. "The Semi-Pro Team that Beat the Champs." In *Baseball in Chicago*. Chicago: Regional Chapter of the Society for American Baseball Research, 1986.

Shiffert, John. *Baseball in Philadelphia*. Jefferson, N.C.: McFarland, 2006.

Simon, Thomas. *Deadball Stars of the National League*. Dulles, Va.: Potomac Books, 2004.

Sinkevitch, Alice. *AIA Guide to Chicago*. Orlando, Fla.: Harcourt Books, 2004.

Sloan, David, and Lisa Parcell. *American Journalism: History, Principles, Practices*. Jefferson, N.C.: McFarland, 2002.

Snyder, John. *Cubs Journal: Year by Year & Day by Day with the Chicago Cubs since 1876*. Cincinnati: Clerisy Press, 2005.

Sokolik, Maggie. "Out of Left Field: Baseball and American Idiom." In *Cooperstown: Symposium on Baseball and American Culture*, edited by Alvin L. Hall. Westport, Conn.: Meckler, 1989.

Spalding, Albert. *America's National Game: Historic Facts Concerning the Beginning, Evolution, Development, and Popularity of Base Ball*. New York: American Sports Publishing, 1911.

Spink, Alfred. *The National Game: A History of Baseball*. St Louis: National Game Publishing, 1910.

Stout, Glenn. *The Cubs: The Complete Story of Chicago Cubs Baseball*. New York: Houghton Mifflin, 2007.

Sugar, Bert. *The Great Baseball Players: From McGraw to Mantle*. Mineola, N.Y.: Dover Publications, 2007.

Sullivan, Dean. *Early Innings: A Documentary History of Baseball, 1825–1908*. Lincoln: University of Nebraska Press, 1995.

Tanner, Eileen. *The Historical Medical Campus at the University of Illinois at*

Chicago: History and Self-Guided Tour of the Oldest Buildings and Grounds at UIC. Chicago: University of Illinois at Chicago, 2012.

Thompson, Gare. *The Southeast: Its History and its People.* Independence, Ky.: National Geographic School Publishing, 2003.

Van Dyne, Edith. *Aunt Jane's Nieces and Uncle John.* Chicago: Reilly & Britton, 1911.

Voigt, David Quentin. *Baseball: An Illustrated History.* University Park: Penn State University Press, 1987.

Wright, Marshall. *Nineteenth Century Baseball: Year-by-Year Statistics for the Major League Teams, 1871 through 1900.* Jefferson, N.C.: McFarland, 1996.

Yardley, Jonathan, ed. *Selected Stories, Ring Lardner.* New York: Penguin Books, 1997.

ARCHIVAL SOURCES

Chicago Cubs cash book, 1876–1881, Chicago History Museum.

Chicago Cubs Correspondence, Chicago History Museum.

Hulbert Family Papers, Chicago History Museum.

Kuhn scrapbooks, Chicago History Museum.

National League Ball Club's records, Chicago History Museum.

Proceedings of the City Council, Chicago History Museum.

U.S. Census Office, 11th Census, 1890, Part I, Part II, Chicago History Museum.

INDEX

Born and raised in France, **LAURENT PERNOT** came to the U.S. as a Chicago-area foreign-exchange student in 1988 and caught '89 Cubs playoff fever. He is the executive vice chancellor of the City Colleges of Chicago and lives in the city with his wife Jennifer and sons Gabriel, Luca, and Leo.

The University of Illinois Press
is a founding member of the
Association of American University Presses.

Designed by Jim Proefrock
Composed in 10.5/13 Bulmer
with Brothers display
at the University of Illinois Press
Manufactured by Sheridan Books, Inc.

University of Illinois Press
1325 South Oak Street
Champaign, IL 61820-6903
www.press.uillinois.edu